FAULT IDENTIFICATION, ANALYSIS, REMEDIAL ACTION AND CONSEQUENCES FOR COMMON DRIVER FAULTS

2ND EDITION

ADI TRAINING FAULT ANALYSIS AND CORRECTION

KATHLEEN KIRKLAND ADI

ALSO SUGGESTED QUESTION AND ANSWERS

Contents

How this book is set out	3
PART ONE	4
Controls and main driving aids	5
Moving off and stopping	13
Reverse around a corner	22
Turn in the road	26
Reverse Parking	30
Controlled emergency stop and use of mirrors	33
Approaching junctions to turn left and right	36
Emerging T Junctions	41
Cross roads	45
Pedestrian Crossings and use of signals	51
Meet Cross and Overtake	53
PART TWO	61
Reverse Parking into a bay	62
Reverse Parking on the road	63
Q&A Judging speed and making normal progress	64
Q&A Approaching junctions	65
Q&A Emerging T Junctions	68
Q&A Crossroads	70
Q&A Pedestrian crossings and use of signals	73
Q&A Meet, cross and overtake	75
Q&A Giving correct signals	78
Q&A Progress, hesitancy and normal stop position	79
Q&A Comprehension of traffic signs	81
Copyright	83

How this book is written

Thank you for purchasing this book. I have written it as an ORDIT trainer with my years of knowledge teaching learners and training ADI's.

This book is written in two parts. The first part looks at **Fault Analysis** and how to remedy them. This book contains over 300 common driver faults that a pupil can make during a lesson. Each fault has a suggested **Identification, Analysis, Remedial action** and a **Consequence** of the error.

The second section has suggested **Questions and Answers** of common faults.

You need to understand how to **Identify** and **Analyse** each driver fault and how to **Remedy** them sufficiently that your instructions are understood. It is not enough to say, 'You steered wide around the corner.' You must Identify the error and **Analyse** why it occurred and how to rectify the error from happening again. When correcting faults, you need to be sure that you;

IDENTIFY: the fault – WHAT did they do?
ANALYSE: the fault – WHY did they do it?
REMEDY: the fault – HOW they can correct it?
CONSEQUENCES: of the fault – WHAT can go wrong?

How to get the most from this book
To get the most from this book, you should familiarize yourself with the faults that a pupil can commit and how to correctly; **Identify, Analyse** and **Remedy**. Using this fault analysis in your everyday teaching or training will become easier to **Analyse** faults that occur.

I hope you find the book helpful. If you have any suggestions or comments, please get in touch with me. I am always looking for input from my readers. I am also available to offer one to one training if required.

PART ONE
FAULT IDENTIFICATION

This section contains over 300 driver faults that a pupil can make during a lesson.

For each driver fault, you must; **Identify**, **Analyse**, **Remedy** and discuss the **Consequences**.

IDENTIFY: the fault – WHAT did they do?
ANALYSE: the fault – WHY did they do it?
REMEDY: the fault – HOW they can correct it?
CONSEQUENCES: of the fault – WHAT can go wrong?

Controls and main driving aids

DOOR

Identify: Kathleen, the door is on the catch.
Analyse: This is because you have not shut the door firmly enough.
Remedy: You must ensure that both hands are on the door and pull the door firmly towards you.
Consequences: The door can ope n whilst driving along.

Identify: Kathleen, the door is on the catch.
Analyse: This is because you never checked after you closed the door.
Remedy: You must push on the door after closing it to be sure it is shut correctly.
Consequences: The door can open whilst you are driving along.

Identify: Kathleen, the interior light is still illuminated in the car.
Analyse: This is because the door is not shut correctly.
Remedy: You must push on the door after closing it to be sure it is shut correctly.
Consequences: The door can open whilst you are driving along.

SEAT

Identify: Kathleen, you are too far/close to the steering wheel.
Analyse: This is because you have not adjusted your seat correctly.
Remedy: You must keep your right hand on the steering wheel and then adjust the leaver under your seat until your left foot is slightly bent when the clutch pedal is depressed fully.
Consequences: Being positioned incorrectly, you will not have the correct amount of car control.

Identify: Kathleen, you do not have control over the seat whilst moving it into position.
Analyse: You are not using the steering wheel to steady yourself whilst adjusting the seat.
Remedy: You must place your right hand on the steering wheel to gain complete control as you operate the seat.
Consequences: You will struggle to adjust your seat effectively.

Identify: Kathleen, you are too close/too far from the steering wheel.
Analyse: This is because you need to adjust the angle of the seat.
Remedy: To adjust the seat, you need to twist the lever on the right-hand side of the seat base.
Consequences: You will not have effective control of the steering wheel if you are too close or far.

Identify: Kathleen, you are too low/high in your seat.
Analyse: This is because you have not adjusted the seat's height.
Remedy: You can adjust the seat height with the lever at the seat's base on the right-hand side.

Consequences: You will not have effective control of the steering wheel if you are too close or far.

HEAT RESTRAINT

Identify: Kathleen, the head restraint will not protect you in the event of a shunt.
Analyse: This is because you have not adjusted the head restraint correctly.
Remedy: You must ensure that at least the top of the head restraint is level with the top of your ears.
Consequences: If you were involved in a collision, there is a greater risk of whiplash if the head restraint is not adjusted correctly.

SEAT BELT

Identify: Kathleen, the seat belt is not flat to your body.
Analyse: This is because you have the seat belt twisted.
Remedy: You need to remove the seat belt and start again.
Consequences: In the event of a collision, the seatbelt would cut into your body, and the inertia will not be effective.

Identify: Kathleen, you have plugged your seat belt into the wrong clip.
Analyse: This is because you have used the clip on the passenger side and not the clip on the driver side.
Remedy: You must ensure that you secure the seat belt to the clip nearest to your seat.
Consequences: In the event of a collision, inertia will not be effective.

Identify: Kathleen, you didn't remove the seat belt correctly and safely.
Analyse: This is because you let go of the seat belt and let it fly back.
Remedy: You must ensure that you remove the seat belt while holding the buckle, take off some slack, and feed it back into the holder, ensuring the buckle does not hit the glass or yourself.
Consequences: Letting the seatbelt fly back could cause damage to yourself or the window.

STEERING WHEEL

Identify: Kathleen, you do not have proper steering wheel control.
Analyse: This is because you have not adjusted the steering wheel height adjuster correctly.
Remedy: You operate the steering wheel's height by using the lever under the steering wheel.
Consequences: You will not have effective control of the steering wheel if you are too close or far.

Identify: Kathleen, your hands are not positioned correctly.
Analyse: They are positioned too low/left/right.
Remedy: You must place your hands at either ten to two or quarter to three positions on the steering wheel. Keep your right hand on the right-hand side of the wheel and your left hand on the left-hand side of the wheel.

Consequences: Crossing your hands over the steering wheel can cause injury if the airbag was to deploy.

MIRRORS

Identify: Kathleen, you are moving your body to see what is in your exterior mirrors.
Analyse: This is because you have not adjusted them correctly.
Remedy: You must be sat back in your seat at your normal driving position as you adjust your mirror.
Consequences: You will not have a complete vision behind you if the mirror is not set correctly.

Identify: Kathleen, you are moving your body to see what is in your interior mirrors.
Analyse: This is because you adjusted them out of sequence.
Remedy: Remember DSSSM. If you adjust your mirror before your seat, you will not have the correct view.
Consequences: You will not have an effective vision behind you if the mirror is not set correctly.

ACCELERATOR

Identify: Kathleen, you are not pressing the gas pedal.
Analyse: This is because you are not pressing the pedal on the far right.
Remedy: Swivel your foot between the brake and gas pedal using your right foot.
Consequences: The car will not move forwards unless you press the gas pedal to put fuel into the engine.

Identify: Kathleen, the car is not moving.
Analyse: This is because you are not injecting fuel into the engine.
Remedy: You need to press your right foot onto the gas pedal.
Consequences: Vehicles behind can be confused why you are not moving.

FOOTBRAKE

Identify: Kathleen, the car is not slowing down.
Analyse: This is because you are not pressing the brake pedal.
Remedy: Using your right foot, you must press the brake to slow the car down.
Consequences: The car will not slow down or stop unless you press the brake pedal.

Identify: Kathleen, the car stopped too sharply.
Analyse: This is because you used the wrong amount of pressure.
Remedy: You need to brake progressively, braking gently at first and then applying more pressure and easing off the pressure as the car comes to a stop.
Consequences: You could cause a rear-end collision by braking too sharply.

Identify: Kathleen, the car stopped too sharply.
Analyse: This is because you used your left foot to operate the brake pedal.
Remedy: You need to use the brake pedal with your right foot.
Consequences: You could cause a rear-end collision by braking too sharply.

Identify: Kathleen, the car stopped too sharply.
Analyse: This is because you used too much pressure on the brake when you depressed the clutch.
Remedy: You need to brake progressively, braking gently at first and then applying more pressure. The clutch and brake pedal require different amounts of pressure applied simultaneously.
Consequences: You could cause a rear-end collision by braking too sharply.

CLUTCH

Identify: Kathleen, the car has stalled.
Analyse: This is because you did not depress the clutch when the car came to a stop.
Remedy: Using your left foot, press the pedal on the far left, leaving your heel on the floor as you operate the clutch pedal.
Consequences: You could cause a rear-end collision by stopping too sharply.

Identify: Kathleen, the car has stalled.
Analyse: This is because you are sitting too far back from the steering wheel and cannot reach the clutch pedal to have complete control.
Remedy: You must adjust your seat correctly to reach all controls once the car is secured.
Consequences: You could cause a rear-end collision by stopping too sharply.

Identify: Kathleen, the car is not driving smoothly.
Analyse: You do not have control of the clutch pedal.
Remedy: You need to keep your left heel on the floor whilst operating the clutch pedal for maximum control.
Consequences: You could cause a rear-end collision by stopping too sharply.

Identify: Kathleen, the car has stalled.
Analyse: This is because you had your left foot on the brake pedal.
Remedy: You must use your right foot to operate the brake and then the left foot for the clutch pedal.
Consequences: You could cause a rear-end collision by stopping too sharply.

HAND BRAKE

Identify: Kathleen, the car is still moving after you have stopped.
Analyse: This is because you have not secured the handbrake securely.

Remedy: You must ensure that you push the button in and pull the hand brake up as far as it will go, releasing the button before releasing the hand brake.
Consequences: The car can roll into another vehicle or another road user if you do not secure the car.

Identify: Kathleen, the car is not moving.
Analyse: This is because you have not removed the handbrake entirely.
Remedy: You must ensure that you push the button in and release the hand brake to the floor.
Consequences: You will not have control of the vehicle if the rear wheels are locked with the hand brake.

Identify: Kathleen, the car is making an audible sound.
Analyse: This is because you have not removed the hand brake entirely.
Remedy: You must ensure that you push the button in and release the hand brake to the floor.
Consequences: You will not have control of the vehicle if the rear wheels are locked with the hand brake.

Identify: Kathleen, the handbrake made a loud noise when you applied it.
Analyse: This is because you did not press the button first.
Remedy: You must press the button at the end of the handbrake before applying it.
Consequences: You can damage the hand brake cable by not pressing the button before applying.

GEARS

Identify: Kathleen, you have selected 3rd gear instead of 1st gear.
Analyse: This is because you have not placed your palm in the correct position.
Remedy: You must ensure that you push your palm away from you with your thumb facing downwards and push the gear lever forwards for 1st gear.
Consequences: The car will not move as effectively in a too lower gear for the car's speed. You can cause another vehicle behind you to collide if you are not moving.

Identify: Kathleen, you have selected the 4th gear instead of 2nd.
Analyse: This is because you have not placed your palm in the correct position.
Remedy: You must ensure that you push your palm away from you with your thumb facing downwards and push the gear lever down for 2nd gear.
Consequences: You can cause the following vehicle to collide with you as your speed will drop suddenly without any warning of brake lights to following vehicles.

Identify: Kathleen, you have selected the 1st gear instead of 3rd.
Analyse: This is because you have not placed your palm in the correct position.
Remedy: You must ensure that your palm is on top of the gear lever and push the lever forward to select 3rd gear.

Consequences: You can cause the following vehicle to collide with you as your speed will drop suddenly without any warning of brake lights to following vehicles.

Identify: Kathleen, you have selected the 2nd gear instead of 4th.
Analyse: This is because you have not placed your palm in the correct position.
Remedy: You must ensure that your palm is on top of the gear lever, and you pull the lever backwards to select 4th gear.
Consequences: You can cause the following vehicle to collide with you as your speed will drop suddenly without any warning of brake lights to following vehicles.

Identify: Kathleen, you have selected the 3rd gear instead of 5th.
Analyse: This is because you have not placed your palm in the correct position.
Remedy: You must ensure that your palm is facing towards with your thumb facing upwards and then push the gear lever towards you and up to select 5th gear.
Consequences: You can cause the following vehicle to collide with you as your speed will drop suddenly without any warning of brake lights to following vehicles.

Identify: Kathleen, you have selected the 4th gear instead of 6th.
Analyse: This is because you have not placed your palm in the correct position.
Remedy: You must ensure that your palm is facing towards with your thumb facing upwards and then push the gear lever towards you and down to select 6th gear.
Consequences: You can cause the following vehicle to collide with you as your speed will drop suddenly without any warning of brake lights to following vehicles.

Identify: Kathleen, you have not selected reverse gear correctly.
Analyse: This is because you have not engaged the button.
Remedy: You must ensure that you engage the button under the gear lever before selecting.
Consequences: The car can stall trying to move into a higher gear and not reverse.

Identify: Kathleen, you have no awareness of the road ahead.
Analyse: This is because you are looking at the gear lever as you select gear.
Remedy: You must ensure that your eyes are on the road ahead at all times when selecting gear.
Consequences: You can collide with another road user if you are not looking where you are going.

Identify: Kathleen, the car made a crunch as you selected gear.
Analyse: This is because you did not depress the clutch pedal fully before selecting the gear.
Remedy: You must depress the clutch pedal fully to the floor before selecting the gear.

Consequences: You can damage the clutch pedal and gear box by not pressing the clutch pedal fully before selecting gear.

Identify: Kathleen, you have not selected reverse gear correctly.
Analyse: This is because you tried to select reverse from a forward gear.
Remedy: You must ensure that the gear lever is neutral first before selecting reverse gear.
Consequences: You can damage the clutch pedal and gear box by not allowing the car to slow first before selecting reverse gear.

STEERING

Identify: Kathleen, you have little control over the steering wheel.
Analyse: This is because you have your hands in the incorrect position.
Remedy: You must ensure that your hands are placed correctly on the steering wheel, at either ten to two or quarter to three positions on the steering wheel.
Consequences: You can injure yourself if the airbag deploys.

Identify: Kathleen, you have little control over the steering wheel.
Analyse: This is because you are only using one hand.
Remedy: You must ensure that you have both your hands placed on the wheel at either ten to two or a quarter to three positions on the steering wheel.
Consequences: If you need to steer quickly, you will not have complete control of the steering wheel if you only use one hand.

Identify: Kathleen, you have little control over the steering wheel.
Analyse: This is because you have your right arm rested on the doorframe.
Remedy: You must have both arms inside the car and your hands placed on the wheel at either ten to two or quarter to three positions on the steering wheel.
Consequences: If you need to steer quickly, you will not have complete control of the steering wheel if you only use one hand.

Identify: Kathleen, you have little control over the steering wheel.
Analyse: This is because you are not holding the steering wheel firmly.
Remedy: You must hold the steering wheel with a firm grip as if holding a child's hand, not too tight but not too loose either.
Consequences: If you need to steer quickly, you will not have complete control of the steering wheel if you are not gripping correctly.

Identify: Kathleen, you have little control over the steering wheel.
Analyse: This is because you are holding the steering wheel too tightly.
Remedy: You must hold the steering wheel with a firm grip as if holding a child's hand, not too tight but not too loose either.
Consequences: If you need to steer quickly, you will not have complete control of the steering wheel if you are not gripping correctly.

INDICATORS

Identify: Kathleen, you have not put the indicators on.

Analyse: This is because you have operated the windscreen wipers.
Remedy: You must ensure that you operate the stalk on the left-hand side of this car.
Consequences: You need to alert other road users of your intentions before you turn; this can cause a collision with another road user if they do not know which direction you are turning.

Identify: Kathleen, the vehicle behind thinks you intend to turn left/right.
Analyse: This is because you have operated the stalk in the wrong direction as if you intend to turn right/left.
Remedy: You must ensure that you operate the stalk on the left-hand side of this car, up to signal right and down to signal left, so the following vehicles are aware of our intentions.
Consequences: You can cause another motorist to collide with you if you are signalling one way and turning the other.

Identify: Kathleen, other road users, think you are turning left.
Analyse: This is because you have not cancelled your signal from the last turning.
Remedy: You must ensure that you cancel your signal once you have turned.
Consequences: You can cause another motorist to collide with you if you have not cancelled your signal.

Moving off and stopping

STARTING

Identify: Kathleen, the engine has not started.
Analyse: This is because you have not turned the key entirely.
Remedy: You must ensure that you operate the key correctly, turning it through all three positions.
Consequences: You will not be able to move the car if it is not switched on.

Identify: Kathleen, the car lurched forwards as you started the engine.
Analyse: This is because you have not selected neutral before starting the engine.
Remedy: You must ensure that the handbrake is secured and the gear lever is neutral before starting the engine.
Consequences: You can collide with another road user if you are not in control of the vehicle when you are starting.

Identify: Kathleen, the engine is not running.
Analyse: This is because you didn't leave the key in the third position long enough.
Remedy: You must ensure the car has started before letting go of the key.
Consequences: The car will not move if the engine is not running.

Identify: Kathleen, the car made a screeching sound.
Analyse: This is because you held the key on the third position too long.
Remedy: You must ensure that you let go of the key once the car has started.
Consequences: You can damage the starter motor if you do not release the key once the car has started.

MIRRORS, VISION AND USE

Identify: Kathleen, the vehicle coming up behind had to swerve to avoid you pulling away from the side of the road.
Analyse: This is because you saw the vehicle but didn't act on what you saw.
Remedy: If a vehicle is approaching, you must wait until it has passed before attempting to pull out if it is closer than ten car lengths away.
Consequences: The vehicle could collide with you if you do not act correctly on what you see in your mirrors.

Identify: Kathleen, you didn't notice the car pulling off his driveway.
Analyse: This is because you didn't check all around you before pulling away from the side of the road.
Remedy: Before you pull away, you must carry out your six-point check. Starting with your left blind spot, left exterior mirror in front of you, exterior mirror, right door mirror and right blind spot.

Consequences: The vehicle could collide with us if you do not make effective observations.

Identify: Kathleen, you never noticed the pedestrian about to cross the road.
Analyse: This is because you did not use your six-point check in the correct order.
Remedy: Before you pull away, you must carry out your six-point check. Starting with your left blind spot, left exterior mirror in front of you, exterior mirror, right door mirror and right blind spot.
Consequences: You could collide with another road user if you don't carry out a 6 point check in the correct order.

MIRRORS; CHANGIN DIRECTION, OVERTAKING AND STOPPING (DOS).

Identify: Kathleen, the vehicle coming up behind had to swerve to avoid you pulling away from the side of the road.
Analyse: This is because you pulled out without checking your mirrors.
Remedy: Before you wish to change direction, you must mirror, signal, then manoeuvre.
Consequences: The vehicle could collide with you if you do not act correctly on what you see.

Identify: Kathleen, the cyclist behind you, had to brake sharply.
Analyse: This is because you pulled around the parked vehicle without checking your mirrors.
Remedy: Before you wish to overtake a parked vehicle, you must mirror, signal then manoeuvre, ensuring there are no other road users.
Consequences: The cyclist could collide with you if you do not act correctly on what you see.

Identify: Kathleen, the vehicle coming up behind had to swerve to avoid you as you pulled into stop.
Analyse: This is because you didn't check your mirrors before stopping.
Remedy: Before you intend to stop, you must ensure that you check your mirrors first to see the following distance of the vehicles behind you.
Consequences: The vehicle could collide with us if you do not check your mirrors correctly and act on what you see.

MIRROR SIGNAL MANOEUVRE.

Identify: Kathleen, you did not check your mirrors before signalling.
Analyse: This is because you are not using MSM in the correct sequence.
Remedy: You need to check your mirrors first, signal, and manoeuvre. You need to be aware of what is around you before you signal your intention.
Consequences: The vehicle could collide with us if you do not check your mirrors correctly and act on what you see.

Identify: Kathleen, you are signalling then checking your mirrors.
Analyse: This is because you are not using MSM in the correct sequence.

Remedy: You need to check your mirrors first, signal, and manoeuvre. You need to be aware of what is around you before you signal your intention.
Consequences: The vehicle could collide with us if you do not check your mirrors correctly and act on what you see.

Identify: Kathleen, the vehicle behind, had to break sharply.
Analyse: This is because you assume that the vehicle behind will slow down.
Remedy: You need to check your mirrors first and adjust your breaking; depending on how close the vehicle follows behind, you may have to break sooner and slower.
Consequences: The vehicle could collide with us if you do not check your mirrors correctly and act on what you see.

Identify: Kathleen, you did not check your mirrors before speeding up.
Analyse: This is because you assumed that the vehicle behind would stay behind you.
Remedy: You need to check your mirrors first as some vehicles may decide to overtake, and you must ease off the gas and let them overtake before increasing your speed.
Consequences: The vehicle could collide with us if you do not check your mirrors correctly and act on what you see.

Identify: Kathleen, you failed to see the vehicle approaching from behind.
Analyse: This is because you did not use your mirrors correctly.
Remedy: You must ensure that you carry out a mirror, signal, and then manoeuvre before changing any direction or speed on the road.
Consequences: The vehicle could collide with us if you do not check your mirrors correctly and act on what you see.

Identify: Kathleen, the vehicle behind, failed to know what you were doing.
Analyse: This is because you did not signal your intention.
Remedy: You must ensure that you carry out a mirror, signal, and then manoeuvre before changing any direction or speed on the road.
Consequences: The vehicle could collide with us if you do not signal your intentions.

Identify: Kathleen, the vehicle behind you was unsure of your intention.
Analyse: This is because you signalled but did not proceed.
Remedy: You must ensure that you only do so when you signal when it is safe to proceed and not before you intend to move off.
Consequences: The vehicle could collide with us if you do not signal your intentions.

Identify: Kathleen, you didn't see the car following us too closely.
Analyse: This is because you failed to check your mirrors before signalling.
Remedy: You must remember MSM and use it in the correct order.
Consequences: The vehicle could collide with us if you do not check your mirrors correctly and act on what you see.

Identify: Kathleen, you pulled away when it wasn't safe.
Analyse: This is because you did your six-point check in the incorrect order.
Remedy: You must carry out your six-point check in the correct order by checking; nearside blind spot, nearside mirror, front windscreen, rearview mirror, offside mirror then your blind spot.
Consequences: The vehicle could collide with us if you do not correctly carry out your six-point check and act on what you see.

PRECAUTIONS BEFORE MOVING OFF.

Identify: Kathleen, the car is not moving.
Analyse: This is because this gear is in neutral.
Remedy: You must ensure that you select first gear before finding the biting point.
Consequences: The car will not move if the vehicle is not in gear.

Identify: Kathleen, the car is not moving.
Analyse: This is because you still have the handbrake applied.
Remedy: You must ensure that you remove the handbrake before attempting to pull away.
Consequences: The car will not move if the hand brake is applied.

Identify: Kathleen, you pulled out when it wasn't safe.
Analyse: This is because you failed to carry out your observations correctly.
Remedy: Before you pull away from the side of the road, you must carry out a six-point check to ensure it is safe to proceed.
Consequences: The vehicle could collide with us if you do not correctly carry out your six-point check and act on what you see.

Identify: Kathleen, you pulled away when it wasn't safe.
Analyse: This is because you didn't act correctly on the situation.
Remedy: You must act on the traffic situation. If the vehicle is at least ten car lengths back, it is safe to proceed. Any closer than that, you should wait.
Consequences: You can collide with a vehicle if you do not act on what you see in your mirrors.

Identify: Kathleen, you pulled away when it wasn't safe.
Analyse: You did not do your six-point check in the incorrect order.
Remedy: You must carry out your six-point check in the correct order by checking; nearside blind spot, nearside mirror, front windscreen, rearview mirror, offside mirror then your blind spot.
Consequences: You could have pulled away into the path of another road user.

COORDINATION OF CONTROLS

Identify: Kathleen, you have stalled the car.
Analyse: This is because you brought the clutch up too quickly.

Remedy: You must slowly bring the clutch up from bite point until the two engine plates couple and coax together.
Consequences: You risk another vehicle driving into the rear of you if you attempt to move off and stall.

Identify: Kathleen, you have stalled the car.
Analyse: This is because you were in the wrong gear.
Remedy: You must select first gear when moving off from a stationary position.
Consequences: You can collide with another vehicle if you attempt to move off and stall.

Identify: Kathleen, you stalled the car.
Analyse: This is because you tried to move off with the hand brake still secured.
Remedy: You must prepare the hand brake before moving off and releasing it before attempting to move.
Consequences: You can collide with another vehicle if you attempt to move off and stall.

Identify: Kathleen, the car didn't pull away smoothly.
Analyse: You didn't use your clutch and gas correctly.
Remedy: You must slowly bring your clutch up and gently operate the gas pedal.
Consequences: You can collide with another vehicle if you attempt to move off and stall.

Identify: Kathleen, you stalled the car.
Analyse: This is because you removed your hand brake, rolled backwards and brought the clutch up too quickly to try and compensate.
Remedy: You must bring the clutch to the bite point, set the gas and then remove the handbrake.
Consequences: You can collide with another vehicle if you attempt to move off and roll back and stall.

Identify: Kathleen, the car is not moving.
Analyse: This is because you have not selected first gear.
Remedy: You must depress your clutch and select first gear for the car to move.
Consequences: The car will not move if you do not select 1st gear.

Identify: Kathleen, you are moving very slowly.
Analyse: This is because you still have the clutch depressed.
Remedy: Once the car moves, you can slowly release the clutch pedal, enabling the car to drive.
Consequences: You can collide with another vehicle if you do not progress after pulling away.

Identify: Kathleen, the car is making a loud noise.
Analyse: This is because you have the gas pedal pressed too hard.
Remedy: You only need to apply light pressure to the gas pedal.
Consequences: You will not have complete control over the vehicle if you press the gas pedal too hard.

Identify: Kathleen, you are driving on the pavement/wrong side of the road.
Analyse: This is because you have not operated the steering wheel the correct amount.
Remedy: You must steer; five minutes to the right, ten minutes to the left and five minutes to the right to your safety line.
Consequences: You can collide with another road user if you are not driving in the centre of your lane.

Identify: Kathleen, the engine made a loud noise.
Analyse: This is because you did not take your foot off the gas when you changed gear.
Remedy: You must take your foot off the gas when you change gear as you are trying to put more fuel into the engine whilst the engine is disconnected.
Consequences: You will not completely control the car if you attempt to change gear with the gas pedal depressed.

Identify: Kathleen, the car veered onto the wrong side of the road.
Analyse: This is because you looked at the gear lever when you changed gear.
Remedy: You must ensure that you look up the road when you change gear.
Consequences: You can collide with another road user if you are not driving in the centre of your lane.

Identify: Kathleen, the gearbox made a loud crunching noise.
Analyse: This is because you did not depress the clutch when you changed gear.
Remedy: You must depress the clutch before you change gear.
Consequences: You can damage the clutch if you do not depress the pedal before changing gear.

Identify: Kathleen, you are not in gear. You are still in neutral.
Analyse: This is because you did not depress the clutch when you changed gear.
Remedy: You must depress the clutch before you change gear.
Consequences: The car will not move if you do not press the clutch pedal before changing gear. The car will stay neutral and slow and collide with another vehicle.

Identify: Kathleen, the car has lost too much speed.
Analyse: This is because you took too long to bring the clutch up after you changed gear.
Remedy: Once you have selected the new gear, you need to slowly bring the clutch up and press your foot back on the gas.
Consequences: The car can stall and collide with another vehicle if you slow down without warning the following vehicle.

Identify: Kathleen, the car lurched forward when you changed gear.
Analyse: This is because you brought the clutch up too quickly after selecting the new gear.

Remedy: You must slowly bring the clutch up once you have changed gear.
Consequences: You can collide with another vehicle as you can stall and come to a sudden stop.

Identify: Kathleen, the car is not driving in a straight line.
Analyse: This is because you are gripping the steering wheel too tightly.
Remedy: You need to use a light but firm grip.
Consequences: You will not have complete control of the steering.

Identify: Kathleen, the car is not driving in a straight line.
Analyse: This is because your hands are incorrectly positioned.
You need to hold the steering wheel at either ten to two or quarter
Remedy: to three for maximum control.
Consequences: You will not have complete control of the steering.

STEERING

Identify: Kathleen, the car is not driving in a straight line.
Analyse: This is because you were moving the steering wheel too much in each direction.
Remedy: The car has power-assisted steering; therefore, you only need to move the steering lightly in each direction.
Consequences: You can cause the car to lose control if you are moving the steering wheel too sharply.

Identify: Kathleen, the car is veering too much towards the middle of the road/kerb.
Analyse: This is because you are concentrating on oncoming traffic.
Remedy: You need to look up the lane you are driving in, scanning far away and back towards you.
Consequences: You can collide with another vehicle if you are not looking where you want to be.

Identify: Kathleen, you lost control of the car.
Analyse: This is because you let the steering wheel slip through your hands.
Remedy: You must use both hands to control the steering wheel using the push and pull method.
Consequences: You will not have complete control over the steering if you need to react quickly.

NORMAL STOP POSITION

Identify: Kathleen, the car is in the incorrect stop position.
Analyse: This is because you are too far out from the kerb.
Remedy: You must ensure that you pull the car back into the kerb, turning five minutes to the left, ten minutes to the right and then five minutes to the left, before stopping.
Consequences: You are giving a misleading signal to other road users.

Identify: Kathleen, the car is in the incorrect stop position.
Analyse: This is because you are too close to the kerb.

Remedy: You must ensure that you pull the car back into the kerb, turning five minutes to the left, ten minutes to the right and then five minutes to the left, before stopping.
Consequences: You can damage the tyres or steering.

Identify: Kathleen, the car is in an inconvenient stop position.
Analyse: This is because you have stopped in front of a driveway.
Remedy: You must ensure that you decide where a safe, legal and convenient place is to stop before you pull up on the side of the road.
Consequences: You have not stopped in a convenient place for drivers wishing to use the driveway.

Identify: Kathleen, the car is stopped in a dangerous position.
Analyse: This is because you have stopped close to a bend.
Remedy: You must ensure that you decide where a safe, legal and convenient place is to stop before you pull up on the side of the road.
Consequences: Drivers coming around the bend may not see you parked there.

Identify: Kathleen, the car is stopped in an illegal position.
Analyse: This is because you have stopped on zig-zag lines.
Remedy: You must ensure that you decide where a safe, legal and convenient place is to stop before you pull up on the side of the road.
Consequences: It is an offence to stop on zig-zag lines.

NORMAL STOP CONTROL

Identify: Kathleen, the car has stalled.
Analyse: You did not operate the brake and clutch pedal correctly.
Remedy: When stopping, you must depress the brake pedal slowly and progressively with your right foot and just before the car comes to a stop, depress the clutch pedal with your left foot to the floor quickly. Then just as the car stops, you can remove your foot from the brake pedal.
Consequences: The following vehicle could collide with you as you come to a stop without warning.

Identify: Kathleen, the car lurched forwards as you stopped.
Analyse: This is because you pressed the brake pedal too sharply once you applied the clutch pedal.
Remedy: When stopping, you must depress the brake pedal slowly and progressively and just before the car comes to a stop, depress the clutch pedal to the floor with your left foot quickly. Just as the car comes to a stop, remove your right foot from the brake pedal.
Consequences: The following vehicle could collide with you as you come to a stop without warning.

Identify: Kathleen, you took too long to bring the car to a stop.
Analyse: This is because you pressed the clutch pedal before the brake pedal.
Remedy: You must brake progressively first, then just before the car comes to a stop, depress the clutch pedal to the floor.
Consequences: You will not fully control the car if the clutch pedal is depressed too early.

Identify: Kathleen, the back wheels locked up when you stopped.
Analyse: This is because you applied the hand brake before the car was entirely stationary.
Remedy: You must keep both hands on the wheel as you brake, and only once the car is stationary can you apply the hand brake and select neutral.
Consequences: The rear brakes will be applied, and the front will keep moving.

Identify: Kathleen, you didn't secure the car safely after stopping.
Analyse: This is because you selected neutral then applied the hand brake.
Remedy: You must apply the hand brake to secure the car, then select neutral.
Consequences: The vehicle could roll back.

Reverse around a corner

COORDINATION OF CONTROLS

Identify: Kathleen, the car travelled too fast.
Analyse: This is because you didn't control the car's speed.
Remedy: You need to have correct clutch control. Slowly bring the clutch pedal up and down the thickness of a pound coin to increase and decrease the speed.
Consequences: You will not have time to control your steering if you travel too fast.

Identify: Kathleen, the car travelled too slow.
Analyse: This is because you didn't control the car's speed.
Remedy: You need to have correct clutch control. Slowly bring the clutch pedal up and down the thickness of a pound coin to increase and decrease the speed.
Consequences: You could dry steer if the car is not moving and damage the tyres or steering.

Identify: Kathleen, the car is not moving.
Analyse: This is because you haven't released the handbrake.
Remedy: Before you start to move, you must release the handbrake.
Consequences: You could dry steer if the car is not moving and damage the tyres or steering.

Identify: Kathleen, the car is not moving.
Analyse: This is because you are pressing the footbrake.
Remedy: Before moving, you must move your feet from the brake pedal onto the gas pedal.
Consequences: The car will stall.

OBSERVATIONS

Identify: Kathleen, you failed to see that vehicle approaching.
Analyse: This is because you are not looking around effectively whilst reversing.
Remedy: You need to ensure that you look backwards and look all around during the manoeuvre, checking for other traffic.
Consequences: You could collide with another vehicle if you are not looking effectively.

Identify: Kathleen, you moved, and a vehicle was approaching.
Analyse: This is because you didn't check to see if it was safe before starting the manoeuvre.
Remedy: You must carry out your six-point check before moving off, and if any vehicles are approaching, you must wait until it is safe.
Consequences: You could collide with another vehicle if you are not looking effectively.

Identify: Kathleen, you moved, and a vehicle was approaching.

Analyse: This is because you made your observations correctly but didn't act on what you saw.
Remedy: If a vehicle is approaching that you can see, you must wait until it has passed and is safe to start the manoeuvre.
Consequences: You could collide with another vehicle if you are not looking effectively.

Identify: Kathleen, you moved, and a vehicle was approaching.
Analyse: This is because you didn't check to see if it was safe after you had started moving.
Remedy: You must look up and down the road whilst moving the car.
Consequences: You could collide with another vehicle if you are not looking effectively.

Identify: Kathleen, you moved, and a vehicle was approaching.
Analyse: This is because you misjudged the speed and distance of the approaching vehicle.
Remedy: If anything is approaching, wait to check their speed and distance.
Consequences: You could collide with another vehicle if you are not looking effectively.

Identify: Kathleen, you travelled backwards in a dangerous manner.
Analyse: This is because you were looking forwards as you travelled.
Remedy: You must look out the rear window between the two seats as you reverse.
Consequences: You could collide with another vehicle if you are not looking effectively.

Identify: Kathleen, you travelled backwards in a dangerous manner.
Analyse: This is because you were looking in your mirrors as you travelled.
Remedy: You must look out the rear window between the two seats as you reverse.
Consequences: You could collide with another vehicle if you are not looking effectively.

Identify: Kathleen, you travelled backwards in a dangerous manner.
Analyse: This is because you were not watching the waiting vehicle, which continued to move as you manoeuvred backwards.
Remedy: You must look up and down the road also.
Consequences: You could collide with another vehicle if you are not looking effectively.

Identify: Kathleen, you gave a dangerous signal to another road user.
Analyse: This is because you waived a road user passed.
Remedy: You must wait and let other road users make their minds about moving.
Consequences: You could be waiving them into danger.

Identify: Kathleen, you gave a dangerous signal to another road user.
Analyse: This is because you waived a pedestrian across the road.

Remedy: Wait and let the pedestrian make their own decision to cross the road.
Consequences: You could be waiving them into danger.

ACCURACY

Identify: Kathleen, the car is too wide as you completed the reverse around the corner.
Analyse: This is because you are not following the kerb line as you are reversing.
Remedy: You need to keep the kerb line in the rear nearside window as you follow the kerb.
Consequences: You could collide with another vehicle if you do not keep to your side of the road.

Identify: Kathleen, the car is too close as you completed the reverse around the corner.
Analyse: This is because you are not following the kerb line as you are reversing.
Remedy: You need to keep the kerb line in the rear nearside window as you follow the kerb.
Consequences: You can damage the tyres and steering.

Identify: Kathleen, the car snaked around the corner.
Analyse: This is because you are not following the kerb line as you are reversing.
Remedy: You need to keep the kerb line in the rear nearside window as you follow the kerb.
Consequences: You could collide with another vehicle if you do not keep to your side of the road.

Identify: Kathleen, the car mounted the kerb as you reversed around the corner.
Analyse: This is because you are not following the kerb line as you are reversing.
Remedy: You need to keep the kerb line in the rear nearside window as you follow the kerb.
Consequences: You can damage the tyres and steering.

Identify: Kathleen, the car is on the right-hand side of the road.
Analyse: This is because you are not following the kerb line as you are reversing.
Remedy: You need to keep the kerb line in the rear nearside window as you follow the kerb.
Consequences: You could collide with another vehicle if you do not keep to your side of the road.

Identify: Kathleen, the car is not straight to the kerb.
Analyse: This is because you brought the car around accurately but did not straighten the car once you were around.
Remedy: You need to wait until the kerb line is in the centre of the rear window and then straighten the wheel.

Consequences: You could collide with another vehicle if you do not keep to your side of the road.

Identify: Kathleen, the car is not straight to the kerb.
Analyse: This is because you brought the car around accurately, but you took too much steering off after turning the car once you were around.
Remedy: You need to wait until the kerb line is in the centre of the rear window and then straighten the wheel. Taking as much steering off as you turned to get around the corner.
Consequences: You could collide with another vehicle if you do not keep to your side of the road.

Turn in the road

CO-ORDINATION OF CONTROLS

Identify: Kathleen, you stalled the engine.
Analyse: This is because you took your foot off the clutch too quickly.
Remedy: You must raise the clutch pedal slowly and use clutch control to control the car's speed.
Consequences: You can hit the kerb, damaging the tyres or steering.

Identify: Kathleen, you stalled the engine.
Analyse: This is because you didn't have your foot on the gas pedal.
Remedy: You must set the gas before moving off.
Consequences: You can hit the kerb, damaging the tyres or steering.

Identify: Kathleen, you stalled the engine.
Analyse: This is because you selected the wrong gear.
Remedy: You must start the manoeuvre in first gear and the second part of the manoeuvre in reverse.
Consequences: You can hit the kerb, damaging the tyres or steering.

Identify: Kathleen, you stalled the engine.
Analyse: This is because you didn't remove the handbrake.
Remedy: You must remove the handbrake before the car starts to move.
Consequences: You can hit the kerb, damaging the tyres or steering.

Identify: Kathleen, the car rolled in between moves.
Analyse: This is because you didn't apply the handbrake.
Remedy: You must secure the car between moves by applying the handbrake.
Consequences: You can hit the kerb, damaging the tyres or steering.

OBSERVATIONS

Identify: Kathleen, you moved when a vehicle was approaching.
Analyse: This is because you did not check to see if it was safe before starting the manoeuvre.
Remedy: You must carry out your six-point check before moving off, and if any vehicle approaches, you must wait until it is safe.
Consequences: You can collide with another vehicle if you do not make observations effectively.

Identify: Kathleen, you moved, and a vehicle was approaching.
Analyse: This is because you made your observations correctly but didn't act on what you saw.
Remedy: If a vehicle is approaching that you can see, you must wait until it has passed or is safe to start the manoeuvre.
Consequences: You can collide with another vehicle if you do not make observations effectively.

Identify: Kathleen, you moved, and a vehicle was approaching.

Analyse: This is because you did not check to see if it was safe in between moves.
Remedy: You must look up and down the road before starting the next part of the manoeuvre.
Consequences: You can collide with another vehicle if you do not make observations effectively.

Identify: Kathleen, you moved, and a vehicle was approaching.
Analyse: This is because you misjudged the speed and distance of the approaching vehicle.
Remedy: If anything is approaching, you must wait to check the speed and distance of the approaching vehicle.
Consequences: You can collide with another vehicle if you do not make observations effectively.

Identify: Kathleen, you travelled backwards in a dangerous manner.
Analyse: This is because you were looking forwards as you travelled.
Remedy: You must look out the rear window between the two seats as you reverse.
Consequences: You can collide with another vehicle if you do not make observations effectively.

Identify: Kathleen, you travelled backwards in a dangerous manner.
Analyse: This is because you were looking in your mirrors as you travelled.
Remedy: You must look out the rear window between the two seats as you reverse.
Consequences: You can collide with another vehicle if you do not make observations effectively.

Identify: Kathleen, you travelled backwards in a dangerous manner.
Analyse: This is because you were looking over your shoulder as you travelled.
Remedy: You must look out the rear window between the two seats as you reverse.
Consequences: You can collide with another vehicle if you do not make observations effectively.

Identify: Kathleen, you travelled backwards in a dangerous manner.
Analyse: This is because you were not watching that waiting vehicle, who decided to move as you travelled.
Remedy: You must look up and down the road also.
Consequences: You can collide with another vehicle if you do not make observations effectively.

Identify: Kathleen, you gave a signal to another road user.
Analyse: This is because you waived a road user passed.
Remedy: You must wait and let other road users make their minds about moving. You could be waiving them into danger.
Consequences: You could waive them into a dangerous situation.

Identify: Kathleen, you gave a dangerous signal to another road user.
Analyse: This is because you waited too long to carry on.

Remedy: If the other driver has decided to wait, then carry on the manoeuvre, keeping a watch on them. You are giving them confusing signals by waiting.
Consequences: You could waive them into a dangerous situation.

Identify: Kathleen, you bumped the kerb.
Analyse: This is because you didn't stop in time.
Remedy: You need to be sure you judge the distance accurately.
Consequences: You can damage the tyres or steering.

Identify: Kathleen, you bumped the kerb.
Analyse: This is because you didn't control the car correctly.
Remedy: You manoeuvred too quickly.
Consequences: You can damage the tyres or steering.

ACCURACY

Identify: Kathleen, you took more turns than necessary.
Analyse: This is because you didn't steer briskly enough.
Remedy: You need to use more significant movements around the steering wheel, allowing you to obtain full lock quicker.
Consequences: It will take you longer and more moves to complete the turn.

Identify: Kathleen, you took more turns than necessary.
Analyse: You didn't steer in the opposite direction as the car got close to the kerb.
Remedy: When you are around one metre from the kerb, you must steer in the opposite direction, removing some steering in preparation for obtaining a full lock in the opposite direction.
Consequences: It will take you longer and more moves to complete the turn.

Identify: Kathleen, you took more turns than necessary.
Analyse: This is because you didn't steer in the opposite direction when you went backwards.
Remedy: When you are around halfway over the road, you must steer in the opposite direction, removing some steering in preparation for obtaining a full lock in the opposite direction.
Consequences: It will take you longer and more moves to complete the turn.

Identify: Kathleen, you took more turns than necessary.
Analyse: This is because you went too fast.
Remedy: You must control the car using clutch control to move the car slowly.
Consequences: It will take you longer and more moves to complete the turn.

Identify: Kathleen, you took more turns than necessary.
Analyse: This is because you didn't consider the camber.
Remedy: You need to assess the steepness of the camber and make allowances for the steepness.

Consequences: It will take you longer and more moves to complete the turn.

Identify: Kathleen, you took more turns than necessary.
Analyse: This is because you started the manoeuvre too far away from the kerb.
Remedy: When you start, you need to be as close to the kerb as you can, so you have the maximum width of the road to use.
Consequences: It will take you longer and more moves to complete the turn.

Identify: Kathleen, you are steering, but the car is not moving.
Analyse: This is because you are steering whilst the car is not moving.
Remedy: You must only steer the car when the car is moving.
Consequences: You can damage the tyres or steering.

Identify: Kathleen, you took more moves than necessary.
Analyse: This is because you did not achieve full lock before reaching the middle of the road.
Remedy: You must steer more briskly to achieve full lock before reaching the centre of the road.
Consequences: It will take you longer and more moves to complete the turn.

Identify: Kathleen, you have mounted the kerb.
Analyse: This is because you did not stop before you reached the kerb.
Remedy: You must stop before reaching the kerb to avoid damaging the car or colliding with anyone on the pavement.
Consequences: You can damage the tyres or steering.

Identify: Kathleen, you completed the manoeuvre in too many moves.
Analyse: This is because you did not use the whole road.
Remedy: You must stop just before you reach the kerb.
Consequences: You can damage the tyres or steering.

Identify: Kathleen, you bumped the kerb.
Analyse: This is because you didn't stop in time.
Remedy: You need to be sure you judge the distance accurately.
Consequences: You can damage the tyres or steering.

Identify: Kathleen, you bumped the kerb.
Analyse: This is because you didn't control the car correctly.
Remedy: You manoeuvred too quickly.
Consequences: You can damage the tyres or steering.

Reverse Parking

REVERSE PARKING INTO A BAY

CO-ORDINATING CONTROLS

Identify: Kathleen, the car is moving too quickly.
Analyse: You are not controlling the car with the clutch pedal.
Remedy: You must ensure the clutch pedal is at bite point and move it up the thickness of a pound coin to make the car move.
Consequences: You will not have complete control over the steering.

Identify: Kathleen, the car is not moving.
Analyse: This is because you do not have your clutch pedal engaged.
Remedy: You must ensure the clutch pedal is at bite point and move it up the thickness of a pound coin to make the car move.
Consequences: You will not make the manoeuvre if the car is not moving.

Identify: Kathleen, the car is not moving.
Analyse: This is because you have not engaged a gear.
Remedy: You must ensure you have selected a gear before moving the car.
Consequences: You will not make the manoeuvre if the car is not moving.

Identify: Kathleen, the car is not moving.
Analyse: This is because you still have the handbrake applied.
Remedy: You must ensure you remove the handbrake to enable the car to move.
Consequences: You will not make the manoeuvre if the car is not moving.

OBSERVATIONS

Identify: Kathleen, you failed to notice that vehicle approaching.
Analyse: This is because you are not making effective observations whilst carrying out the exercise.
Remedy: You must ensure you look behind you and all around you whilst carrying out this exercise.
Consequences: You could collide with another vehicle if you are not making effective observations.

ACCURACY

Identify: Kathleen, you are over the white lines.
Analyse: This is because you steered too early/late.
Remedy: You must ensure you start turning at precisely the right point.
Consequences: You could collide with another parked vehicle.

Identify: Kathleen, you are not straight in the bay.
Analyse: This is because you did not straighten the wheels.

Remedy: You must straighten the wheels when the car is straight in the bay.
Consequences: You could collide with another parked vehicle.

PARALLEL PARKING ON ROAD

CO-ORDINATION OF CONTROLS

Identify: Kathleen, the car is moving too quickly.
Analyse: You are not controlling the car with the clutch pedal.
Remedy: You must ensure the clutch pedal is at bite point and move it up the thickness of a pound coin to make the car move.
Consequences: You will not have complete control over the car.

Identify: Kathleen, the car is not moving.
Analyse: This is because you do not have your clutch pedal engaged.
Remedy: You must ensure the clutch pedal is at bite point and move it up the thickness of a pound coin to make the car move.
Consequences: You will not complete the manoeuvre if the car is not moving.

OBSERVATIONS

Identify: Kathleen, you failed to notice that vehicle approaching.
Analyse: This is because you are not making effective observations whilst carrying out the exercise.
Remedy: You must ensure you look behind you and all around you whilst carrying out this exercise.
Consequences: You could collide with another vehicle if you are not making effective observations.

Identify: Kathleen, you were manoeuvring dangerously.
Analyse: This is because you are not making effective observations whilst carrying out the exercise.
Remedy: You must ensure you look behind you and all around you whilst carrying out this exercise.
Consequences: You could collide with another vehicle if you are not making effective observations whilst moving.

ACCURACY

Identify: Kathleen, you are too close to the kerb.
Analyse: This is because you steered too early.
Remedy: You must ensure you start turning at precisely the right point.
Consequences: You will not be parked accurately and can damage the tyres.

Identify: Kathleen, you are too far from the kerb.
Analyse: This is because you steered too late.
Remedy: You must ensure you start turning at precisely the right point.
Consequences: You will not be parked accurately, and another vehicle could collide with yours when parked.

Controlled emergency stop and use of mirrors

QUICK REACTION

Identify: Kathleen, you stopped the car, but it was not firm enough for an emergency.
Analyse: This is because you didn't react quickly enough.
Remedy: You must ensure your reaction pressing the footbrake is quicker.
Consequences: You could collide with the object you are trying to avoid.

Identify: Kathleen, you stopped the car, but it was not firm enough for an emergency.
Analyse: This is because you didn't apply enough pressure onto the footbrake.
Remedy: You must ensure you press firmer on footbrake, much firmer than a regular stop.
Consequences: You could collide with the object you are trying to avoid.

USE OF FOOTBRAKE AND CLUTCH

Identify: Kathleen, you stopped the car, but it was not firm enough for an emergency.
Analyse: This is because you didn't use the footbrake correctly and firmly enough.
Remedy: You must ensure your reaction pressing the footbrake is pressed firmer, firmer than a regular stop.
Consequences: You could collide with the object you are trying to avoid.

Identify: Kathleen, the car took too long to come to a stop.
Analyse: This is because you depressed the clutch simultaneously as the brake pedal.
Remedy: You must ensure that you only use the footbrake to brake and only depress the clutch at the final moment, just as the car is about to come to a stop.
Consequences: You could collide with the object you are trying to avoid.

Identify: Kathleen, the car has stalled.
Analyse: This is because you failed to depress the clutch pedal as the car came to a stop.
Remedy: To prevent the car from stalling, depress the clutch pedal to the floor just before the car comes to a stop.
Consequences: You will not have complete control over the car if the engine stalls.

MIRRORS, VISION AND USE

Identify: Kathleen, you did not check your mirrors before moving away from the side of the road.
Analyse: This is because you did not carry out the MSM before you pulled away from the side of the road.

Remedy: You need to ensure that you carry out your six-point check and signal right before pulling away.
Consequences: You could collide with another vehicle if you do not check your mirrors before pulling away.

Identify: Kathleen, you did not check your mirrors after moving off after performing the emergency stop.
Analyse: This is because you did not carry out the MSM before you pulled away.
Remedy: You need to ensure that you carry out your six-point check and signal right before pulling away because the car is in the middle of the lane/road.
Consequences: You could collide with another vehicle if you do not check your mirrors before pulling away.

Identify: Kathleen, the following vehicle was unsure of your intentions.
Analyse: This is because you did not give a signal to alert other road users of your intentions.
Remedy: You are now in the middle of your lane/road after performing the emergency stop. You need to signal left to inform the following vehicle of your intentions to wait.
Consequences: You could collide with another vehicle if you do not check your mirrors before pulling away.

USE OF MIRRORS.

Identify: Kathleen, you did not check your mirrors before changing Direction/Overtook/Stopped.
Analyse: This is because you did not use MSM.
Remedy: The MSM routine is not just for moving away from the side of the road. You must ensure you use them before changing direction, overtaking and stopping.
Consequences: You could collide with another vehicle if you do not check your mirrors before changing speed, changing direction or stopping.

MIRROR, SIGNAL, MANOEUVRE

Identify: Kathleen, the following vehicle did not know what you were doing.
Analyse: This is because you didn't give a signal to advise the following vehicle.
Remedy: If the vehicle is too close to continue in front of, you must signal left. If you have enough time to continue, you must signal right.
Consequences: You could collide with another vehicle if you do not act correctly on what you see in your mirrors.

Identify: Kathleen, the following vehicle did not know what you were doing.
Analyse: This is because you signalled right to move away, but you stayed stationary.
Remedy: If the following vehicle is too close to pull away, you must wait until the vehicle has passed before signalling.
Consequences: You are giving a confusing signal to other vehicles.

Identify: Kathleen, you pulled out too close to the vehicle approaching in the distance.
Analyse: This is because you did not act and decide on what you saw.
Remedy: You must look, assess and decide when it is safe to pull out.
Consequences: You could collide with another vehicle if you do not act correctly on what you see in your mirrors.

Approaching junctions to turn left and right

MIRRORS

Identify: Kathleen, you did not check your mirrors before signalling.
Analyse: This is because you were looking up the road.
Remedy: You need to be sure to use the MSM, mirror, and signal manoeuvre routine when approaching junctions.
Consequences: You need to know what is behind you, as you could collide with another vehicle if you are not aware they are there.

Identify: Kathleen, the vehicle behind you had to make an emergency stop.
Analyse: This is because you didn't check your mirrors before braking.
Remedy: You need to check how close the following vehicle is before braking as this may need to be sooner and slower to allow the following vehicle time to react.
Consequences: You could collide with the vehicle following you if you do not allow their closeness when braking.

Identify: Kathleen, you did not notice the cyclist on the left-hand side of the car.
Analyse: This is because you didn't check your left-hand door mirror before signalling.
Remedy: You must use your mirrors in pairs. Inside and outside in the direction you are travelling before you signal to check for cyclists.
Consequences: You could collide with the cyclist if you are unaware they are there.

SIGNALS

Identify: Kathleen, the following vehicle did not know you intended to turn right/left.
Analyse: This is because you did not signal your intention.
Remedy: You need to be sure to use the MSM, mirror, and signal and manoeuvre routine on the approach to a junction.
Consequences: You could collide with the vehicle as they are unsure of your intentions.

Identify: Kathleen, you did not MSM in the correct order.
Analyse: This is because you signalled first and checked your mirrors after.
Remedy: You must remember the correct order; mirrors, signal, and manoeuvre.
Consequences: You could collide with another vehicle if you do not check your mirrors to see what is there first.

BRAKES

Identify: Kathleen, the vehicle behind, had to make an emergency stop.
Analyse: This is because you did not use your brake progressively.

Remedy: You must remember the correct way to brake progressively is to apply gentle pressure at first, then increase the pressure, then ease off as the car comes to a stop.
Consequences: You could collide with another vehicle if you do not brake slowly to allow for their closeness.

Identify: Kathleen, the car almost came to a sudden stop when you applied the brakes.
Analyse: This is because you used your left foot to apply the footbrake.
Remedy: You must remember to use your right foot to apply gentle pressure at first, then increase the pressure, then ease off as the car comes to a stop.
Consequences: The following vehicle could collide if you come to a sudden stop.

Identify: Kathleen, you are not slowing the car down quick enough.
Analyse: This is because you are not pressing the brake pedal firmly enough.
Remedy: You must remember the correct way to brake progressively is to apply gentle pressure at first, then increase the pressure, then ease off as the car comes to a stop.
Consequences: You could collide with what is in front of you if you do not brake progressively enough.

GEARS

Identify: Kathleen, the car juddered after you changed gear.
Analyse: You selected 4th gear and not 2nd gear from 3rd.
Remedy: You must remember to use the palm of your hand to direct the gear lever into the correct position.
Consequences: The car will stall if you are in a higher gear for the speed you are driving.

Identify: Kathleen, the car is struggling to move.
Analyse: This is because you are trying to move off in second gear.
Remedy: You must remember that you need to select first gear to move off again after stopping at the junction.
Consequences: The car will stall if you try to pull away in second gear.

COASTING

Identify: Kathleen, the car sped up as you turned the corner.
Analyse: This is because you kept your left foot on the clutch pedal after you selected second gear.
Remedy: You must ensure that the clutch pedal is up entirely before you start your turning.
Consequences: The car is not completely controlled if you drive whilst your clutch is depressed.

SPEED ON APPROACH TOO FAST/TOO SLOW

Identify: Kathleen, you did not have time to carry out MSM before turning the corner.

Analyse: This is because you approached the junction too fast.
Remedy: You must ensure that you check your mirrors and give a signal. Once you have given information to the following vehicles, you need to ease off the gas to let the car start to slow down, then apply the brakes.
Consequences: You will not have complete control of the car as you turn if you are travelling too fast.

Identify: Kathleen, the following vehicle overtook you dangerously.
Analyse: This is because you approached the junction too slow.
Remedy: You must ensure that you check your mirrors and give a signal around five car lengths from the junction and then start slowing down.
Consequences: The vehicle overtaking could collide with another vehicle whilst overtaking.

Identify: Kathleen, the following vehicle was unsure of your actions.
Analyse: The following vehicle thought that you were slowing down to stop at the side of the road.
Remedy: You must ensure that you check your mirrors and give a signal around five car lengths from the junction and then start slowing down.
Consequences: The following vehicle could collide with us if it thought you were stopping and we kept going.

STEERING

Identify: Kathleen, you mounted the kerb as you entered the last junction.
Analyse: This is because you started steering too soon.
Remedy: You must ensure that you follow the kerb line around as you approach.
Consequences: You can damage the tyres and steering of the car if you mount the kerb.

PEDESTRIANS

Identify: Kathleen, you didn't notice the pedestrian already crossing the road you were entering.
Analyse: This is because you didn't look into the road before you turned.
Remedy: You must ensure no pedestrians or obstructions in the junction you are about to enter. You must give way to pedestrians already crossing.
Consequences: You could collide with a pedestrian.

Identify: Kathleen, you put the pedestrian into a dangerous position.
Analyse: This is because you invited them to cross the road.
Remedy: You must ensure they make up their mind to cross.
Consequences: You can waive them into danger.

CROSS APPROACHING TRAFFIC

Identify: Kathleen, you caused the approaching vehicle to slow down.
Analyse: This is because you miss-judged the speed of the vehicle approaching.
Remedy: You must ask yourself, would you walk across the road in front of the oncoming vehicle. If you would, there is enough time.

Consequences: You can collide with the vehicle you are crossing in front of.

Identify: Kathleen, you have made the following vehicles wait unnecessarily.
Analyse: This is because you had more than enough time to emerge from the junction.
Remedy: You must ask yourself, would you walk across the road in front of the oncoming vehicle. If you would, there is enough time.
Consequences: Other vehicles may overtake you in a dangerous position.

RIGHT CORNER CUT

Identify: Kathleen, you were on the wrong side of the road when you turned right.
Analyse: This is because you didn't position the car correctly before you turned.
Remedy: You must ensure that you do not start steering into the turning until the car's front is level with the centre of the road you are turning into.
Consequences: You could collide with a vehicle coming in the opposite direction.

Identify: Kathleen, you were on the wrong side of the road when you turned right.
Analyse: This is because you oversteered as you came out of the junction.
Remedy: You must ensure that you start to straighten the steering when the car is three-quarters of the way into the lane.
Consequences: You could collide with a vehicle coming in the opposite direction.

Identify: Kathleen, you mounted the kerb when you turned right.
Analyse: This is because you started steering too late.
Remedy: You must ensure that you start to steer into the junction when the car's front is level with the middle of the road you are turning into.
Consequences: You could collide with a vehicle coming in the opposite direction.

JUDGING SPEED AND MAKING PROGRESS

Identify: Kathleen, you are driving too slow.
Analyse: This is because you didn't notice the speed limit sign change as you turned.
Remedy: When entering a new road, you need to look for any change of speed limit.
Consequences: You could force other motorists to overtake when it may not be safe.

Identify: Kathleen, you are driving too fast.
Analyse: This is because you didn't notice the speed limit sign change as you turned.

Remedy: When entering a new road, you need to look for any change of speed limit.
Consequences: You could harm another motorist; if you are travelling too fast, they may pull out in front of you, thinking they have time.

Identify: Kathleen, you did not notice the cyclist on the left-hand side of the car.
Analyse: This is because you didn't check your left-hand door mirror before signalling.
Remedy: You must use your mirrors in pairs. Inside and outside in the direction you are travelling before you signal to check for cyclists.
Consequences: You could collide with the cyclist if you are unaware they are there.

ROAD POSITIONING

Identify: Kathleen, you are driving too close to the kerb.
Analyse: You are not looking far enough up the road.
Remedy: You need to look where you want the car to go.
Consequences: You could bump the kerb and cause a puncture.

Identify: Kathleen, you are driving too far from the kerb.
Analyse: You are not looking far enough up the road.
Remedy: You need to look where you want the car to go.
Consequences: You could collide with another motorist, being too close to the centre of the road.

Identify: Kathleen, you are not driving in the correct lane.
Analyse: This is because you did not look at the road markings.
Remedy: You need to look at the road markings.
Consequences: You could collide with another motorist if you drive in the wrong lane.

Identify: Kathleen, you are straddling your lane.
Analyse: This is because you did not look at the road markings.
Remedy: You need to look at the road markings.
Consequences: You could collide with another motorist if you straddle into another lane.

Emerging T Junctions

MIRROR, SIGNAL, MANOEUVRE

Identify: Kathleen, you signalled before; you checked your mirrors.
Analyse: This is because you did not carry out the correct sequence, MSM.
Remedy: You must carry out mirror, signal, then manoeuvre in the correct order to alert other road users of your intentions.
Consequences: If the following vehicle follows too closely, they could collide with you.

Identify: Kathleen, the vehicle following us, had to brake sharply.
Analyse: This is because you did not apply your signal before braking.
Remedy: You must check your mirrors and signal your intentions to turn to other road users.
Consequences: If the following vehicle follows too closely, they could collide with you.

Identify: Kathleen, the following vehicle almost overtook you.
Analyse: This is because you started signalling too early, and the following vehicle thought you were pulling over.
Remedy: You need to check your mirrors and start signalling around five car lengths from the junction.
Consequences: The following vehicle that overtook you could collide with you.

Identify: Kathleen, the vehicle following us, had to brake sharply.
Analyse: This is because you did not check your mirrors on the approach to the crossing.
Remedy: You need to scan the pavement on the approach, as you may need to stop, but first check your mirrors to see if anyone is following closely and adjust your braking as to how close the following vehicle is.
Consequences: The following vehicle could collide with you, and you risk colliding with the pedestrian on the crossing.

Identify: Kathleen, the following vehicle had to brake suddenly.
Analyse: This is because you didn't signal your intentions to turn.
Remedy: You need to check your mirrors and signal before you start braking.
Consequences: The following vehicle could collide with you if you do not give a signal.

SPEED

Identify: Kathleen, you emerged from that junction very fast.
Analyse: This is because you did not apply the foot brake before emerging.
Remedy: You must remember MSPSL to reduce your speed before turning.
Consequences: You can lose control and collide with another vehicle.

Identify: Kathleen, you emerged from that junction very slow.
Analyse: This is because you did not bring your clutch up as you turned.
Remedy: Once you have committed to emerging, you must ensure you complete the manoeuvre as quickly and safely as possible.
Consequences: The following vehicle could collide with you if you emerge too slowly.

GEARS

Identify: Kathleen, the car struggled to emerge out of the turning.
Analyse: This is because you emerged from that junction in 3rd gear.
Remedy: You must ensure that you select first gear when you stop before attempting to emerge.
Consequences: You could stall, and the following vehicle could collide with you.

Identify: Kathleen, the car lurched forwards as you emerged.
Analyse: This is because you emerged from that junction in 1st gear.
Remedy: You were still moving, so you should have stayed in 2nd gear.
Consequences: You will not have complete control over the vehicle, and the following vehicle could collide with you.

COASTING

Identify: Kathleen, the car emerged too fast from the junction.
Analyse: This is because after you selected 2nd gear, you kept your clutch down (coasted).
Remedy: You must ensure that once you have selected the appropriate gear, you must slowly bring your clutch up to engage the engine before emerging.
Consequences: You will not have complete control over the vehicle; you could collide with another road user.

Identify: Kathleen, you oversteered as you emerged from the junction.
Analyse: This is because after you selected 2nd gear, you kept your clutch down (coasted).
Remedy: You must ensure that once you have selected the appropriate gear, you must slowly bring your clutch up to engage the engine before emerging.
Consequences: You will not have complete control over the vehicle; you could collide with another road user.

OBSERVATIONS

Identify: Kathleen, you caused the approaching vehicle to change speed.
Analyse: This is because you did not make effective observations before emerging that it was safe to emerge and pulled out in front of the vehicle.
Remedy: You must ensure that it is safe to emerge and not cause another vehicle to change speed or direction. Ask yourself if you would walk across the road safely.
Consequences: You must not cause another road user to change speed or direction. They could collide with you.

Identify: Kathleen, you came too close to the pedal cyclists.
Analyse: This is because you didn't see him in your left-hand mirror.
Remedy: You must use your mirrors in pairs, checking your rearview mirror and left-hand mirror before emerging left.
Consequences: You could collide with the pedal cyclist.

EMERGING

Identify: Kathleen, you emerged unsafely.
Analyse: This is because you could not see before emerging.
Remedy: You need to creep and peep if it is a closed junction or obscured by vehicles.
Consequences: You could emerge into danger.

Identify: Kathleen, the vehicle behind, was unsure why you stopped.
Analyse: The junction is an open junction, and you can see if it is clear on the approach.
Remedy: You need to observe the junction on the approach, either open or closed; if open and clear, you can emerge.
Consequences: The following vehicle could collide with you if you do not emerge when it is safe to do so.

POSITION TO TURN RIGHT

Identify: Kathleen, you emerged on the wrong side of the road.
Analyse: This is because you did not position yourself correctly before emerging.
Remedy: You must position just left of the centre of the road.
Consequences: You could collide with another road user on the other side of the road as you emerge
unsafely.

POSITION TO TURN LEFT

Identify: Kathleen, you mounted the kerb as you emerged.
Analyse: This is because you were not positioned correctly before you emerged.
Remedy: You must ensure that you have followed the kerb line round as you emerge.
Consequences: You could damage the car steering or tyres if you mount the kerb.

PEDESTRIANS

Identify: Kathleen, you didn't notice the pedestrian already crossing the road you were emerging into.
Analyse: This is because you didn't look into the road before you turned.
Remedy: You must ensure no pedestrians or obstructions in the junction you are about to enter. You must give way to pedestrians already crossing.
Consequences: You could collide with the pedestrian.

Identify: Kathleen, you put the pedestrian in danger.

Analyse: This is because you invited them to cross.
Remedy: You must let the pedestrians make their minds regarding crossing.
Consequences: You could be waiving the pedestrians into danger.

Crossroads

MIRROR, SIGNAL, MANOEUVRE

Identify: Kathleen, you did not notice the pedal cyclist on your left.
Analyse: This is because you failed to check your left door mirror before you applied the signal.
Remedy: The routine MSM is the correct procedure. Internal mirror and left door mirror before signalling left. Interior mirror and right door mirror before signalling right.
Consequences: You could collide with the cyclist.

Identify: Kathleen, you did not notice the motorcyclist on your right.
Analyse: This is because you failed to check your right door mirror before you applied the signal.
Remedy: The routine MSM is the correct procedure. Internal mirror and left door mirror before signalling left. Interior mirror and right door mirror before signalling right.
Consequences: You could collide with the motorcyclist.

Identify: Kathleen, the vehicle behind, did not know your intentions.
Analyse: This is because you signalled after you had manoeuvred.
Remedy: You must use Mirror, signal, manoeuvre in the correct sequence.
Consequences: The following vehicle could collide with you if you slow down without warning.

Identify: Kathleen, the vehicle pulling off his driveway thought you were turning right.
Analyse: This is because you signalled right instead of left.
Remedy: You must ensure you signal your intentions correctly to warn other road users.
Consequences: The reversing driver could continue and collide with you.

Identify: Kathleen, you failed to notice the cyclist turning at the junction alongside you.
Analyse: This is because you didn't check your exterior mirror.
Remedy: You must ensure you use your exterior mirror in conjunction with your interior mirror.
Consequences: You could collide with the cyclist.

Identify: Kathleen, you held up the traffic unnecessarily at the junction.
Analyse: This is because you signalled left but failed to go when it was clear to do so.
Remedy: You must ensure you manoeuvre when it is safe.
Consequences: The following vehicle could collide with you if you do not emerge with you when it is safe to do so.

Identify: Kathleen, the vehicle behind, was unsure of your intentions.
Analyse: This is because you did not signal before you started slowing.
Remedy: You must ensure you carry out MSM in the correct order.
Consequences: The following vehicle could collide with you if you start

slowing without giving a signal.

SPEED

Identify: Kathleen, you approached the crossroad junction too fast.
Analyse: This is because you applied the foot brake too late.
Remedy: You need to use the footbrake sooner and progressively. A suggestion would be three car lengths sooner.
Consequences: You could stop over the line and stop in the path of oncoming vehicles.

Identify: Kathleen, you are positioned too far over the give way lines.
Analyse: This is because you misjudged where the lines are.
Remedy: You need to look at the lines as you approach.
Consequences: Stopping over the give way lines means you are stopping in the path of oncoming vehicles.

Identify: Kathleen, you are positioned too far from the give way lines.
Analyse: This is because you misjudged where the lines are.
Remedy: You need to look at the lines as you approach.
Consequences: The following vehicle may overtake you and drive into danger.

Identify: Kathleen, you approached the crossroad junction too slow.
Analyse: Because you started braking too early.
Remedy: Start braking around five car lengths from the junction.
Consequences: The following vehicle may overtake you and drive into danger.

GEARS

Identify: Kathleen, you stalled as you emerged at the crossroad.
Analyse: This is because you tried to pull away in 3rd gear.
Remedy: Be sure to select 1st and not 3rd, push the gear lever away from you and up to ensure you do not select the wrong gear.
Consequences: You can stall, and the following vehicle could collide with you.

Identify: Kathleen, you have stalled the car emerging from the junction.
Analyse: This is because you were in the incorrect gear.
Remedy: You must ensure that you select first gear before pulling away when you are stationary.
Consequences: The following vehicle could collide with you if you stall.

Identify: Kathleen, the car was not under control as you turned.
Analyse: This is because you were in the incorrect gear.
Remedy: You must ensure that your gear matches your speed before you make your turn.
Consequences: You will not control the car if you are in the incorrect gear.

COASTING

Identify: Kathleen, the car sped up.
Analyse: This is because you left your clutch down after selecting the correct gear.
Remedy: Be sure to release the clutch pedal fully after selecting a gear.
Consequences: You will not have complete control of the car.

Identify: Kathleen, the car sped up.
Analyse: This is because you had your clutch pedal depressed as you made the turning.
Remedy: You must ensure that you have selected the correct gear and your clutch is up entirely before starting the turn.
Consequences: You will not have complete control of the car.

Identify: Kathleen, the car sped up as you approached the junction.
Analyse: This is because you had your clutch pedal depressed whilst breaking.
Remedy: You only need to depress the clutch pedal before stopping or changing gear.
Consequences: You will not have complete control of the car.

OBSERVATIONS

Identify: Kathleen, you didn't look as you entered the crossroad junction.
Analyse: You only looked forwards and to your left/right.
Remedy: Be sure to make effective observations at a crossroads before you are sure it is safe to emerge. Looking forwards, right, left, right, left and forwards.
Consequences: You could drive into a dangerous situation and have a collision.

Identify: Kathleen, you failed to notice the obstruction as you entered the junction.
Analyse: This is because you did not make effective observations before turning.
Remedy: You must ensure that you look both ways and into the junction you are turning into before making the turn to ensure it is safe to proceed.
Consequences: You could collide with the obstruction.

EMERGING

Identify: Kathleen, you emerged unsafely at the crossroad junction.
Analyse: This is because you misjudged the speed of the oncoming traffic.
Remedy: You need to LOOK, ASSESS, DECIDE and ACT on what you see. If in doubt, hang about.
Consequences: You could collide with the oncoming vehicle.

Identify: Kathleen, you cannot see the road you are entering enough.
Analyse: You are positioned too far behind the give way lines.
Remedy: You must look at the give way lines as you approach; this will ensure you stop at the give way white lines and not before them.
Consequences: The following vehicle could overtake you dangerously if you stop too far from the give way lines.

Identify: Kathleen, you almost knocked the cyclist off.
Analyse: This is because you didn't take effective observations before turning.
Remedy: You must look into the junction before turning to check for cyclists and pedestrians.
Consequences: You could collide with the cyclist.

POSITION FOR TURNING RIGHT

Identify: Kathleen, you emerged onto the wrong side of the road.
Analyse: This is because you steered too soon.
Remedy: You need to steer once the car is in the new road, not before.
Consequences: You could collide with a vehicle coming in the opposite direction.

Identify: Kathleen, the vehicle behind is unsure of your intention.
Analyse: This is because you are positioned too far over to the left with your right signal applied.
Remedy: You must stop just left of the centre of the road if you intend to turn right.
Consequences: The vehicle behind could overtake you dangerously.

Identify: Kathleen, you came very close to the vehicle approaching as you turned.
Analyse: This is because you were in the middle of the road over the white lines as you emerged.
Remedy: You need to position yourself within your lane to emerge safely.
Consequences: You could collide with a vehicle coming in the opposite direction.

POSITION FOR TURNING LEFT

Identify: Kathleen, you mounted the kerb as you emerged left.
Analyse: This is because you straightened up too late.
Remedy: You must straighten the steering wheel when two-thirds of the way around the turning.
Consequences: You could damage the steering or tyres if you hit the kerb.

Identify: Kathleen, you cannot see enough of the road you are turning into.
Analyse: This is because you are positioned too far over to the right.
Remedy: You must stop, following the kerb line around, giving you a wider field of vision of the road you are about to enter.
Consequences: You could emerge into the path of another vehicle.

Identify: Kathleen, you mounted the kerb as you turned.
Analyse: This is because you started steering too early.
Remedy: You must ensure that you start steering once the front of your car is level with the kerb line.

Consequences: You could damage the steering or tyres if you hit the kerb.

Identify: Kathleen, you entered the road on the wrong side of the road.
Analyse: This is because you started steering too late.
Remedy: You must ensure that you start steering once the front of your car is level with the kerb line.
Consequences: You could collide with an oncoming vehicle if you emerge onto the wrong side of the road.

PEDESTRIANS

Identify: Kathleen, you didn't give way to the pedestrians crossing the mouth of the crossing.
Analyse: This is because you weren't unaware that you had to.
Remedy: The Highway Code says that pedestrians have priority if they are already crossing the road you intend to turn into.
Consequences: You could collide with the pedestrians.

Identify: Kathleen, you failed to notice the pedestrian crossing.
Analyse: This is because you did not make effective observations before turning.
Remedy: You must ensure that you look both ways and into the junction you are turning into before making the turn to ensure it is safe to proceed.
Consequences: You could collide with the pedestrians.

Identify: Kathleen, you put that pedestrian in a dangerous situation.
Analyse: This is because you invited them to cross.
Remedy: You must let them make their mind up about crossing the road. You could be waiving them into danger. Make eye contact to see their intentions.
Consequences: You could waive them into danger.

CROSSING APPROACHING TRAFFIC

Identify: Kathleen, you crossed the approaching traffic unsafely.
Analyse: This is because you misjudged the speed of the approaching traffic.
Remedy: Use the guideline; if you could walk across safely, you could drive across safely.
Consequences: You must not cause another vehicle to change speed or direction.

Identify: Kathleen, you caused the approaching vehicle to change its speed.
Analyse: This is because you turned too soon.
Remedy: Ask yourself whether you would walk across the road.
Consequences: You must ensure that you do not cause other vehicles to slow down or change direction.

Identify: Kathleen, you waited unnecessarily before turning across the traffic.

Analyse: This is because you miss judged the speed of the approaching traffic.
Remedy: You must ensure that you ask yourself would you walk across the road.
Consequences: Another vehicle could overtake you dangerously if you wait when it is safe.

RIGHT CORNER CUTTING

Identify: Kathleen, you cut the corner as you turned right into the junction.
Analyse: This is because you turned too early.
Remedy: Be sure only to turn when the front of your bonnet is level with the centre lines/road you are about to turn into.
Consequences: You could collide with another vehicle if you are driving on the wrong side of the road.

Identify: Kathleen, you almost contacted the vehicle emerging from the junction.
Analyse: This is because you cut the corner of the turning you were entering.
Remedy: You must only turn once the front of your car is level with the front of the centre of the road you are turning into.
Consequences: You could have collided with the vehicle.

Pedestrian Crossings and use of signals

MIRROR, SIGNAL, MANOEUVRE

Identify: Kathleen, the vehicle following us, had to brake sharply.
Analyse: This is because you did not check your mirrors on the approach to the crossing.
Remedy: You need to scan the pavement on the approach, as you may need to stop, but first check your mirrors to see if anyone is following closely and adjust your braking as to how close the following vehicle is.
Consequences: The following vehicle could collide with us if you brake suddenly.

Identify: Kathleen, the following vehicle almost overtook you.
Analyse: This is because you started braking too early for the crossing.
Remedy: You need to check your mirrors before you start braking.
Consequences: The overtaking vehicle could collide with the pedestrians on the crossing.

OBSERVATIONS

Identify: Kathleen, you were not going to stop at the pedestrian crossing.
Analyse: This is because you did not check to see if the crossing was about to be used.
Remedy: You need to scan the pavement on the approach, and if anyone is walking towards the crossing, check your mirrors and start slowing down and be prepared to stop.
Consequences: You could collide with a pedestrian on the crossing.

OVERTAKING

Identify: Kathleen, you MUST NOT overtake a moving vehicle on the zigzag lines approaching the crossing.
Analyse: This is because you did not realise you were approaching a crossing.
Remedy: You must check your road marking before starting an overtake manoeuvre to ensure it is not illegal.
Consequences: It is illegal, and you can be prosecuted for carrying out an overtake on the zig-zag area on either side of the crossing.

INVITING PEDESTRIANS TO CROSS

Identify: Kathleen, you put the pedestrian in danger.
Analyse: This is because you waived them across the road.
Remedy: You must not invite others to cross. Wait and let them make their own decision.
Consequences: You do not want them to be hit by a vehicle coming in the opposite direction.

SIGNALS BY ARM

Identify: Kathleen, you gave an incorrect signal for slowing.

Analyse: This is because you gave the signal for turning left.
Remedy: You need to hold your arm straight and move it up and down clearly.
Consequences: The following vehicle may overtake you.

Identify: Kathleen, you gave an incorrect signal for turning right.
Analyse: This is because you gave a signal for slowing down.
Remedy: You need to hold your right arm straight out of the window.
Consequences: Following vehicles could overtake you.

Identify: Kathleen, you gave an incorrect signal for turning left.
Analyse: This is because you gave the signal for slowing down.
Remedy: You need to hold your left arm straight out of the window and rotate it.
Consequences: The following vehicle may overtake you.

SIGNALS TIMING

Identify: Kathleen, you gave a late signal coming off the roundabout.
Analyse: This is because you gave the signal after leaving the roundabout.
Remedy: You need to signal once you are past the last turning you wish to take.
Consequences: Other vehicles will have to wait unnecessarily until you have exited the roundabout.

Identify: Kathleen, you confused the following vehicle.
Analyse: This is because you gave the signal to turn left too early, and he thought you were pulling over.
Remedy: You need to signal around five car lengths from the turning you intend to turn into.
Consequences: The following vehicle could overtake you.

UNNECESSARY SIGNALS

Identify: Kathleen, you signalled unnecessarily at that junction.
Analyse: Because you were turning left, you had you signalled right.
Remedy: Carry out MSM on the approach to the junction.
Consequences: Other vehicles may overtake you.

Identify: Kathleen, you gave a dangerous left signal.
Analyse: This is because you signalled left to return after you passed the parked car.
Remedy: Any vehicles waiting to emerge may think you are turning left. Only signal when it is appropriate.
Consequences: A vehicle waiting to emerge from the junction may proceed from seeing your left signal.

Meet Cross and Overtake

MIRROR, SIGNAL, MANOEUVRE

Identify: Kathleen, you did not notice the vehicle following closely behind you.
Analyse: This is because you did not carry out a mirror check.
Remedy: You need to remember to carry out MSM before you turn.
Consequences: The vehicle behind could collide with you as they need to take time to react.

Identify: Kathleen, you did not check the correct mirrors before signalling left/right.
Analyse: This is because you failed to check your left/right door mirror.
Remedy: The routine MSM is the correct procedure. Internal mirror and left door mirror before signalling left. Interior mirror and right door mirror before signalling right.
Consequences: You could collide with a cyclist or another road user.

Identify: Kathleen, the vehicle behind, did not know your intentions.
Analyse: This is because you signalled after you had manoeuvred.
Remedy: You must use Mirror, signal, manoeuvre in the correct sequence.
Consequences: The vehicle behind could have collided with us as you slowed without signalling your intention.

Identify: Kathleen, the vehicle pulling off his driveway thought you were turning right.
Analyse: This is because you signalled right instead of left.
Remedy: You must ensure you signal your intentions correctly to warn other road users.
Consequences: You could have collided with the vehicle if they kept reversing.

Identify: Kathleen, you failed to notice the cyclist turning at the junction alongside you.
Analyse: This is because you didn't check your exterior mirror.
Remedy: You must ensure you use your exterior mirror in conjunction with your interior mirror.
Consequences: You could have collided with the cyclist.

Identify: Kathleen, you held up the traffic unnecessarily at the junction.
Analyse: This is because you signalled left but failed to go when it was clear to do so.
Remedy: You must ensure you manoeuvre when it is safe.
Consequences: The following vehicle could have overtaken you dangerously.

Identify: Kathleen, the vehicle behind, was unsure of your intentions.
Analyse: This is because you did not signal before you started slowing.
Remedy: You must ensure you carry out MSM in the correct order.

Consequences: The following vehicle could collide with you if you start slowing without warning.

MEETING APPROACHING TRAFFIC

Identify: Kathleen, you caused that oncoming vehicle to slow down.
Analyse: This is because you didn't give way to the oncoming vehicle.
Remedy: You need to be looking further up the road to see if there are oncoming vehicles and where you can pull in safely to let them pass.
Consequences: You can cause another vehicle to change speed or direction.

Identify: Kathleen, you caused that oncoming vehicle to mount the kerb.
Analyse: This is because you didn't assess the situation ahead. The vehicle was already committed and had nowhere to pull in.
Remedy: You need to be looking further up the road to see if there are oncoming vehicles and where you can pull in safely to let them pass.
Consequences: You could have collided with the oncoming vehicle.

CROSSING TRAFFIC

Identify: Kathleen, you caused the oncoming traffic to slow down.
Analyse: This is because you made an error judging the vehicle's speed and distance.
Remedy: Before you cross the traffic, you need to ask yourself if you would walk across the road in front of the vehicle.
Consequences: You could collide with the vehicle.

OVERTAKING TRAFFIC

Identify: Kathleen, you pulled back in front of the vehicle after overtaking it too closely.
Analyse: This is because you did not check your rearview mirror before pulling back in.
Remedy: You must check your mirrors and ensure the vehicle you are overtaking is fully visible in your rear view mirror before you pull back in.
Consequences: You could have caused the vehicle to change speed or direction.

Identify: Kathleen, the vehicle you overtook had to slow down.
Analyse: This is because you completed the overtaking manoeuvre, but you did not make progress after.
Remedy: Once you have completed the overtake, you must progress up to a safe speed limit.
Consequences: This can cause the following vehicle to change speed or direction.

Identify: Kathleen, you almost knocked the cyclist off his bike.
Analyse: This is because you pulled back in too soon after overtaking them.
Remedy: You need to make sure you can see the cyclist fully in your rearview mirror before pulling back in.

Consequences: Cyclists are very vulnerable, and you can cause them to wobble and maybe fall off.

KEEPING A SAFE DISTANCE

Identify: Kathleen, you are too close to the vehicle in front.
Analyse: This is because you are unaware of your safe distance.
Remedy: You should keep at least a two-second gap from the vehicle you follow in good weather conditions.
Consequences: If the vehicle in front has to make an emergency stop, you will not have enough time to stop behind them.

Identify: Kathleen, you are too close to the vehicle in front.
Analyse: This is because you are unaware of your safe distance.
Remedy: You should keep at least a four-second gap from the vehicle you follow in wet weather conditions.
Consequences: If the vehicle in front has to make an emergency stop, you will not have enough time to stop behind them.

Identify: Kathleen, you are too close to the vehicle in front.
Analyse: This is because you are unaware of your safe distance.
Remedy: You should keep at least a twenty-second gap from the vehicle you follow in icy conditions.
Consequences: If the vehicle in front has to make an emergency stop, you will not have enough time to stop behind them.

Identify: Kathleen, you have stopped too close to the vehicle in front of you whilst waiting in stationary traffic.
Analyse: This is because you have not considered what you would do if you needed to pull around the vehicle.
Remedy: When you pull up, ensure you can see the vehicle's tyres in front and some tarmac.
Consequences: If the vehicle in front breaks down, you will not be able to pull around him.

SHAVING OTHER VEHICLES

Identify: Kathleen, you passed the vehicle too closely.
Analyse: This is because you miss judged the distance away from the vehicle.
Remedy: You should give at least a door width when you pass a vehicle.
Consequences: If the driver opens their door without looking, you could collide with the other person's car door.

ANTICIPATION OF PEDESTRIANS

Identify: Kathleen, you almost run those pedestrians over.
Analyse: This is because you failed to anticipate that they were going to cross.
Remedy: You need to be aware that pedestrians can be unpredictable, wait and allow them to make their mind up if they are going to cross.
Consequences: You could collide with the pedestrians.

Identify: Kathleen, you put those pedestrians in a dangerous situation.
Analyse: This is because you invited them to cross.
Remedy: You need to let pedestrians make their minds up if they cross.
Consequences: You could be waiving them into danger.

ANTICIPATION OF CYCLISTS

Identify: Kathleen, you almost knocked that cyclist off their bike.
Analyse: This is because you failed to anticipate that they would ride in front of you.
Remedy: You need to be aware that cyclists can be unpredictable
Consequences: If the cyclist stops pedalling, it is usually an indication they intend to change direction.

Identify: Kathleen, you almost knocked the cyclist off his bike.
Analyse: This is because you pulled back in too soon after overtaking them.
Remedy: You need to make sure you can see the cyclist fully in your rearview mirror before pulling back in.
Consequences: You could cause the cyclist to wobble and fall off.

Identify: Kathleen, the cyclist, wobbled as you passed them.
Analyse: This is because you did not give him enough room.
Remedy: You must give him at least as much room as you would a car.
Consequences: The cyclist may need to move around a pot-hole or wet drain.

ANTICIPATION OF DRIVERS

Identify: Kathleen, you failed to realise that vehicle was about to emerge from the side road.
Analyse: This is because you failed to anticipate the vehicle's movements.
Remedy: You need to be aware that vehicles can be unpredictable.
Consequences: You could collide with another vehicle if you do not anticipate others.

Identify: Kathleen, you almost emerged from the junction when another vehicle approached.
Analyse: This is because you saw the left-hand signal and assumed they were turning left.
Remedy: You need to pay attention to other vehicles, and if they are approaching too fast, they may have left their indicator on from the last junction.
Consequences: You could emerge into the path of the oncoming car.

GIVING CORRECT SIGNALS

Identify: Kathleen, you signalled in the wrong direction.
Analyse: This is because you did not move the indicator stalk in the direction you wish to travel.
Remedy: You need to remember the indicator stalk moves in the same direction as the steering wheel.

Consequences: The vehicle behind could be confused by your signal and make a wrong move based on your indication.

Identify: Kathleen, the vehicle pulling off his driveway thought you were turning right.
Analyse: This is because you signalled right instead of left.
Remedy: You must ensure you signal your intentions correctly to warn other road users.
Consequences: You could have collided with the vehicle if they kept reversing.

Identify: Kathleen, the vehicle behind, did not know your intentions.
Analyse: This is because you signalled after you had manoeuvred.
Remedy: You must use Mirror, signal, manoeuvre in the correct sequence.
Consequences: The vehicle behind could have collided with us as you slowed without signalling your intention.

Identify: Kathleen, the vehicle pulling off his driveway thought you were turning right.
Analyse: This is because you signalled right instead of left.
Remedy: You must ensure you signal your intentions correctly to warn other road users.
Consequences: You could have collided with the vehicle if they kept reversing.

Identify: Kathleen, you held up the traffic unnecessarily at the junction.
Analyse: This is because you signalled left but failed to go when it was clear to do so.
Remedy: You must ensure you manoeuvre when it is safe.
Consequences: The following vehicle could have overtaken you dangerously.

Identify: Kathleen, the vehicle behind, was unsure of your intentions.
Analyse: This is because you did not signal before you started slowing.
Remedy: You must ensure you carry out MSM in the correct order.
Consequences: The following vehicle could collide with you if you start slowing without warning.

Identify: Kathleen, the vehicle behind, was unsure of your intentions.
Analyse: This is because you signalled unnecessarily around the parked vehicle.
Remedy: When overtaking a parked vehicle, moving out early enough signals to other motorists, you intend to overtake.
Consequences: The following vehicle could overtake you if they think you are turning left after you have completed the overtake.

FLASHING OF HEADLIGHTS

Identify: Kathleen, you flashed your headlights incorrectly.
Analyse: This is because you thought it was a signal to other motorists to proceed.
Remedy: Wait and let the other road users make their minds up.

Consequences: Another motorist, who you haven't seen, may think the flashing is for them, and they could proceed into danger.

Identify: Kathleen, you proceeded dangerously.
Analyse: This is because another vehicle flashed, and you thought it was for you.
Remedy: Flashing is not a signal to go. If someone flashes you, wait to see if the other vehicle stops before proceeding.
Consequences: The other motorists may not be flashing you, and you could collide with another road user if it is unclear.

BRAKE LIGHTS

Identify: Kathleen, the following vehicle didn't know you were slowing.
Analyse: This is because you didn't brake, only slowing with your gears.
Remedy: You must use your foot brake, not just your gears to slow.
Consequences: The following motorist could collide with you.

COMPREHENSION OF TRAFFIC SIGNS

Identify: Kathleen, you are exceeding the speed limit.
Analyse: This is because you didn't see the speed limit sign change.
Remedy: Lookup, most speed limit changes occur on the approach to junctions.
Consequences: You could put another road user in danger.

Identify: Kathleen, you have taken the wrong turning.
Analyse: This is because you didn't read the signpost correctly.
Remedy: Lookup on the approach to junctions to see which turning is correct.
Consequences: You could put another road user in danger by making the wrong turn.

TRAFFIC LIGHTS

Identify: Kathleen, you crossed an amber light.
Analyse: This is because you approached the green light too fast.
Remedy: Check your mirrors on the approach to the green light, ease off and be prepared to stop.
Consequences: You could put another road user in danger.

Identify: Kathleen, you proceeded on, red and amber light.
Analyse: This is because you started before the light had turned green.
Remedy: Do not cross the line until the light is green.
Consequences: You could put another road user in danger.

TRAFFIC CONTROLLERS

Identify: Kathleen, you didn't slow for the temporary traffic lights.
Analyse: This is because you didn't notice the road works sign on the approach.
Remedy: Look further up the road, anticipating any changes.
Consequences: You could put another road user in danger.

Identify: Kathleen, you didn't slow for the traffic controller early enough.
Analyse: This is because you didn't notice the sign for traffic control ahead.
Remedy: Look further up the road, anticipating any changes.
Consequences: You could put another road user in danger.

Identify: Kathleen, you didn't slow for the traffic controller early enough.
Analyse: This is because you didn't notice the sign for traffic control ahead.
Remedy: Look further up the road, anticipating any changes.
Consequences: You could put another road user in danger.

Identify: Kathleen, you didn't slow for the traffic controller early enough.
Analyse: This is because you waited until they stepped in the road.
Remedy: Look further up the road, and start slowing as soon as they hold up their sign.
Consequences: You could put another road user in danger.

GIVE WAY SIGNS

Identify: Kathleen, you were going too fast approaching the give way.
Analyse: This is because you didn't see the give way sign on the approach.
Remedy: Look further up the road and start anticipating changes in the road.
Consequences: You could put another road user in danger.

Identify: Kathleen, you stopped too far from the give way line.
Analyse: This is because you were looking somewhere else on the approach.
Remedy: Look at the give way lines on the approach.
Consequences: You could put another road user in danger.

Identify: Kathleen, you stopped too far over the give way line.
Analyse: This is because you were looking somewhere else on the approach.
Remedy: Look at the give way lines on the approach.
Consequences: You could put another road user in danger.

Identify: Kathleen, you are in the correct lane.
Analyse: This is because you didn't look at the direction sign.
Remedy: Look at the direction sign on the approach to the junction.
Consequences: You could put another road user in danger.

Identify: Kathleen, you are straddling the lane.
Analyse: This is because you are not looking at the road markings.
Remedy: Look at the lane you are driving in.
Consequences: You could put another road user in danger.

Identify: Kathleen, you attempted to enter a no-entry.
Analyse: Because you didn't see the no-entry sign.

Remedy: Look up when turning into a new junction to see the no-entry sign.
Consequences: You could put another road user in danger.

PART TWO

QUESTION AND ANSWER

Here are a selection of question and answers to ask a trained pupil why they made an error.

You do not want to instruct a trained pupil; you want to ask them questions relating to the fault, so they can figure out what they did wrong and correct it from happening again.

Reverse Parking into a bay

CO-ORDINATION OF CONTROLS

Question: Kathleen, why is the car is moving too quickly?
Answer: This is because you are not controlling the car's speed with the clutch pedal.

Question: Kathleen, why is the car not moving?
Answer: You do not have the clutch pedal at the bite point of the clutch pedal.

Question: Kathleen, why is the car not moving?
Answer: This is because you do not have the gear selected to reverse.

Question: Kathleen, why is the car not moving?
Answer: This is because you still have the handbrake applied.

OBSERVATIONS

Question: Kathleen, why did you brake sharply?
Answer: This is because you didn't notice the vehicle approaching.

ACCURACY

Question: Kathleen, why are you over the white lines?
Answer: This is because you didn't steer enough/too much.

Question: Kathleen, why are you not straight in the bay?
Answer: This is because you didn't steer enough/too much.

Reverse Parking on the road

CO-ORDINATION OF CONTROLS

Question: Kathleen, why is the car is moving too quickly?
Answer: This is because you are not controlling the car's speed with the clutch pedal.

Question: Kathleen, why is the car not moving?
Answer: You do not have the clutch pedal at the bite point of the clutch pedal.

Question: Kathleen, why is the car not moving?
Answer: This is because you do not have the gear selected to reverse.

Question: Kathleen, why is the car not moving? (Manual)
Answer: This is because you still have the handbrake applied.

OBSERVATIONS

Question: Kathleen, why did you brake sharply?
Answer: This is because you didn't notice the vehicle approaching.

ACCURACY

Question: Kathleen, why are you too close to the kerb?
Answer: This is because you steered too early.

Question: Kathleen, why are you are too far from the kerb?
Answer: This is because you steered too late.

Q&A Judging speed and making normal progress

DRIVING AT INCORRECT SPEED

Question: Kathleen, why are you driving too slow?
Answer: This is because you didn't notice the speed limit sign change as you turned.

Question: Kathleen, why are you are driving too fast.
Answer: This is because you didn't notice the speed limit sign change as you turned.

OBSERVATIONS

Question: Kathleen, why did you not notice the cyclist on the left-hand side of the car?
Answer: This is because you didn't check your left-hand door mirror before signalling.

Question: Kathleen, why did you not notice the pedestrian stepping into the road?
Answer: This is because you didn't look far enough up the road.

Q&A Approaching junctions

MIRRORS

Question: Kathleen, why did you not check your mirrors before you signalled?
Answer: This is because you checked them simultaneously as you signalled.

Question: Kathleen, did you not check the correct mirrors before signalling?
Answer: This is because you were unaware of the correct mirrors to use before signalling left/right.

Question: Kathleen, why did you not notice the vehicle behind you?
Answer: This is because you did not carry out a mirror check.

Question: Kathleen, why did you not check the correct mirrors before signalling left/right.
Answer: This is because you failed to check your left/right door mirror.

Question: Kathleen, why did you not notice the cyclist on the left-hand side of the car?
Answer: This is because you didn't check your left-hand door mirror before signalling.

SIGNALS

Question: Kathleen, why did the following vehicle not know your intentions to turn?
Answer: This is because you did not signal before you turned.

Question: Kathleen, why did the vehicle pulling off his driveway think you were turning right?
Answer: This is because you signalled right instead of left.

Question: Kathleen, why did the vehicle behind you not know your intentions?
Answer: This is because you signalled after you had turned.

Question: Kathleen, why was the vehicle behind was unsure of your intentions?
Answer: This is because you did not signal before you started slowing.

BRAKES

Question: Kathleen, why did the car travel too fast into the junction?
Answer: You didn't apply enough pressure on the brake pedal.

Question: Kathleen, why did the car travel too slowly into the junction?
Answer: This is because you started braking too early.

GEARS

Question: Kathleen, why did the car struggle to turn into the junction?
Answer: This is because you selected 4th gear and not 2nd.

COASTING

Question: Kathleen, why did the car travel too fast and wide into the junction?
Answer: This is because you kept your clutch pedal down after changing gear (coasted).

Question: Kathleen, why did the car travel too fast and wide into the junction?
Answer: This is because you put your clutch pedal down simultaneously as braking (coasted).

TOO FAST

Question: Kathleen, why were you unable to make effective observations at the junction?
Answer: This is because you approached the junction too fast.

Question: Kathleen, why did the car travel too fast into the junction?
Answer: This is because you didn't change into 2nd gear before turning.

TOO SLOW

Question: Kathleen, why did you approach the junction too slowly?
Answer: This is because you started braking too early.

POSITION

Question: Kathleen, why did you emerge onto the wrong side of the road?
Answer: This is because you positioned yourself to turn right instead of close to the kerb to turn left.

Question: Kathleen, why did you emerge onto the wrong side of the road?
Answer: This is because you positioned yourself to turn left instead of positioning to turn right.

PEDESTRIANS

Question: Kathleen, why did you almost run the pedestrians over as you turned into the junction?
Answer: This is because you did not observe them already crossing the road.

Question: Kathleen, how did you put the pedestrians in a dangerous situation.?

Answer: This is because you invited them to cross the road.

CROSS APPROACHING TRAFFIC

Question: Kathleen, why did you cause the oncoming vehicle to slow down?
Answer: This is because you crossed their path, but there was not enough time.

Question: Kathleen, how did you confuse the following vehicle?
Answer: This is because you had time to emerge but still waited.

RIGHT CORNER CUT

Question: Kathleen, why did you turn into the junction dangerously?
Answer: This is because you cut the corner of the junction as you turned.

Question: Kathleen, why did you almost have a collision with the road user as you turned into the junction?
Answer: This is because you cut the corner as you entered the junction.

Q&A Emerging T Junctions

MIRROR, SIGNAL, MANOEUVRE

Question: Kathleen, why didn't you carry out MSM in the correct order?
Answer: This is because you signalled, then checked your mirrors.

Question: Kathleen, why did you not notice the vehicle behind you?
Answer: This is because you did not carry out a mirror check.

Question: Kathleen, why did you not check the correct mirrors before signalling left/right?
Answer: This is because you failed to check your left/right door mirror.

Question: Kathleen, why did the vehicle behind not know your intentions?
Answer: This is because you signalled after you had turned.

Question: Kathleen, why did the vehicle pulling off his driveway think you were turning right?
Answer: This is because you signalled right instead of left.

Question: Kathleen, why did you fail to notice the cyclist turning at the junction alongside you?
Answer: This is because you didn't check your exterior mirror.

Question: Kathleen, why did you hold up the traffic unnecessarily at the junction?
Answer: This is because you signalled left but failed to go when it was clear to do so.

Question: Kathleen, why was the vehicle behind you unsure of your intentions?
Answer: This is because you did not signal before you started slowing.

SPEED

Question: Kathleen, why did you approach the junction far too fast?
Answer: This is because you didn't use your brakes early enough.

Question: Kathleen, why were you unable to make effective observations at the junction?
Answer: This is because you approached the junction too fast.

Question: Kathleen, why did the car travel too fast into the junction?
Answer: This is because you didn't change into 2nd gear before turning.

Question: Kathleen, why did you approach the junction too slowly?
Answer: This is because you started braking too early.

GEARS

Question: Kathleen, why did the car struggle to turn into the junction?

Answer: This is because you had the car in 3rd gear still.

Question: Kathleen, why did the car struggle to turn into the junction?
Answer: This is because you selected 4th gear and not 2nd.

COASTING

Question: Kathleen, why did you coast as you emerged from the junction?
Answer: This is because you changed gear too late.

OBSERVATIONS

Question: Kathleen, why didn't you look effectively as you entered the crossroad junction?
Answer: This is because you only looked forwards and to your left/right.

Question: Kathleen, why didn't you notice the pedestrians crossing?
Answer: This is because you didn't look in all directions.

EMERGING

Question: Kathleen, why did you emerge from the junction unsafely?
Answer: This is because you misjudged the speed and distance of the approaching traffic on the main road.

POSITION TURNING RIGHT

Question: Kathleen, why were you positioned incorrectly before turning right?
Answer: This is because you didn't move far enough over to the right.

POSITION TURNING LEFT

Question: Kathleen, why did you emerge on the wrong side of the road?
Answer: This is because you did not position yourself correctly.

Question: Kathleen, why did you mount the kerb as you made the turn?
Answer: This is because you steered too early.

PEDESTRIANS

Question: Kathleen, how did you put those pedestrians in danger?
Answer: This is because you waived them across the road.

Q&A Crossroads

MIRROR, SIGNAL, MANOEUVRE

Question: Kathleen, why did not check the correct mirrors before signalling?
Answer: This is because you were unaware of the correct mirrors to use before signalling left/right.

Question: Kathleen, why did you not notice the vehicle behind you?
Answer: This is because you did not carry out a mirror check.

Question: Kathleen, why did you not check the correct mirrors before signalling left/right?
Answer: This is because you failed to check your left/right door mirror.

Question: Kathleen, why did the vehicle behind not know your intentions?
Answer: This is because you signalled after you had turned.

Question: Kathleen, why did the vehicle pulling off their driveway think you were turning left?
Answer: This is because you signalled left instead of right.

Question: Kathleen, why did you fail to notice the cyclist turning at the junction alongside you?
Answer: This is because you didn't check your exterior mirror.

Question: Kathleen, why was the vehicle behind you was unsure of your intentions?
Answer: This is because you did not signal before you started slowing.

SPEED

Question: Kathleen, why did you cut the corner of the junction as you turned?
Answer: This is because you approached too fast.

Question: Kathleen, how did you confuse the driver behind?
Answer: This is because you approached the junction too slow.

GEARS

Question: Kathleen, why did the car stall as you emerged at the crossroad?
Answer: This is because you tried to pull away using the incorrect gear.

COASTING

Question: Kathleen, why did you coast as you turned left/right at the crossroad?
Answer: You left your clutch down after you selected the correct gear.

Question: Kathleen, why did you approach the junction too fast?
Answer: This is because you depressed the clutch pedal as you were braking.

OBSERVATIONS

Question: Kathleen, why didn't you look correctly as you entered the crossroad junction?
Answer: This is because you only looked forwards and to your left/right.

Question: Kathleen, why didn't you notice the pedestrians crossing?
Answer: You didn't look in all directions.

EMERGING

Question: Kathleen, why did you emerge unsafely at the crossroad junction?
Answer: This is because you misjudged the speed of the oncoming traffic.

Question: Kathleen, why did you hold up the traffic unnecessarily at the junction?
Answer: This is because you signalled left but failed to go when it was clear to do so.

POSITION TURN RIGHT

Question: Kathleen, why did you emerge onto the wrong side of the road?
Answer: This is because you steered too soon.

Question: Kathleen, why did you mount the kerb as you entered the road?
Answer: This is because you steered too late.

POSITION TURN LEFT

Question: Kathleen, why did you mount the kerb as you entered the new road after you emerged left?
Answer: This is because you straightened up too late.

Question: Kathleen, why did you enter the new road on the wrong side of the road?
Answer: This is because you started steering too late.

PEDESTRIANS

Question: Kathleen, didn't you give way to the pedestrians crossing the mouth of the crossing?
Answer: This is because you expected them to wait.

Question: Kathleen, why didn't you give way to the pedestrians crossing the mouth of the crossing.

Answer: This is because you were not looking into the road as you turned.

Question: Kathleen, how did you put those pedestrians into a dangerous situation?
Answer: This is because you invited them to cross.

CROSSING APPROACHING TRAFFIC

Question: Kathleen, why did you cross the approaching traffic unsafely?
Answer: This is because you misjudged the speed of the approaching traffic.

Question: Kathleen, why did you wait unnecessarily?
Answer: This is because you missed the safe emerging gap in the traffic.

RIGHT CORNER CUTTING

Question: Kathleen, why did you cut the corner as you turned into the junction?
Answer: This is because you started steering too early.

Question: Kathleen, why did you cut the corner as you turned into the junction?
Answer: This is because you didn't reduce your speed enough before you turned.

Q&A Pedestrian crossings and use of signals

MIRROR, SIGNAL, MANOEUVRE

Question: Kathleen, why did the vehicle following you have to brake sharply?
Answer: This is because you did not check your mirrors on the approach to the crossing, to ascertain how close the vehicle was behind you.

SPEED ON APPROACH

Question: Kathleen, why did you accelerate up to the zebra crossing?
Answer: This is because you did not check to see if the crossing was about to be used.

STOP WHEN NECESSARY (ZEBRA)

Question: Kathleen, why did you are travel too fast to stop at the light-controlled crossing?
Answer: This is because you did not check to see if the crossing was about to be used.

STOP WHEN NECESSARY (LIGHT CONTROL)

Question: Kathleen, why were you not stopping at the light-controlled crossing?
Answer: This is because you did not check to see if the crossing was about to be used, either someone waiting who has pressed the button or someone about to press the button.

OVERTAKING ON APPROACH

Question: Kathleen, why did you attempt to overtake within the zigzag lines on the approach to a pedestrian crossing.
Answer: You must not overtake within the zig-zag lines approaching the crossing.

INVITING PEDESTRIANS TO CROSS

Question: Kathleen, how did you put those pedestrians in danger?
Answer: This is because you thought you were being courteous by waiving them across.

SIGNALS BY ARM

Question: Kathleen, why did you give an incorrect signal for slowing?
Answer: This is because you gave the signal for turning left.

Question: Kathleen, why did you give an incorrect signal for turning left?
Answer: This is because you put your left arm out.

SIGNALS TIMING

Question: Kathleen, why did you give a late signal coming off that roundabout?
Answer: This is because you gave the signal after leaving the roundabout.

Question: Kathleen, why did the vehicle following you think you were taking the exit before the one you did.
Answer: This is because you signalled too early.

UNNECESSARY SIGNALS

Question: Kathleen, why did you give a late signal coming off that roundabout?
Answer: Kathleen, this is because you gave the signal after leaving the roundabout.

Question: Kathleen, why are you confusing other road users with your signals?
Answer: Kathleen, this is because you signalled to leave a mini-roundabout.

Question: Kathleen, why did the vehicle emerge from the junction in front of you?
Answer: This is because you were signalling left after passing a parked vehicle.

Q&A Meet, cross and overtake

MIRROR, SIGNAL, MANOEUVRE

Question: Kathleen, why did you not check the correct mirrors before signalling?
Answer: This is because you were unaware of the correct mirrors to use before signalling left/right.

Question: Kathleen, why didn't you notice the vehicle behind you?
Answer: This is because you did not carry out a mirror check.

Question: Kathleen, why did you not check the correct mirrors before signalling left/right?
Answer: This is because you failed to check your left/right door mirror.

Question: Kathleen, why did the vehicle behind not know your intentions?
Answer: This is because you signalled after you had turned.

Question: Kathleen, why did the vehicle pulling off their driveway think you were turning right.
Answer: This is because you signalled right instead of left.

Question: Kathleen, why did you fail to notice the cyclist turning at the junction alongside you?
Answer: This is because you didn't check your exterior mirror.

Question: Kathleen, why did you hold up the traffic unnecessarily at the junction?
Answer: This is because you signalled left but failed to go when it was clear to do so.

Question: Kathleen, why was the vehicle behind you unsure of your intentions?
Answer: This is because you did not signal before you started slowing.

MEET

Question: Kathleen, why did you not wait behind the obstruction on your side when meeting the oncoming traffic?
Answer: This is because you didn't plan where you would pull in.

Question: Kathleen, why did you not wait behind the obstruction on your side when meeting the oncoming traffic?
Answer: This is because you had room to pull over but did not.

Question: Kathleen, why did you cause the oncoming vehicle to mount the kerb?
Answer: This is because you didn't assess the situation ahead. The vehicle was already committed and had nowhere to pull in, causing them to mount the kerb.

CROSS

Question: Kathleen, why did you cross in front of the oncoming vehicle, causing them to slow down?
Answer: This is because you misjudged its speed and distance.

Question: Kathleen, how have you confused the vehicle behind you?
Answer: This is because you had time to pull out safely into the traffic.

OVERTAKE

Question: Kathleen, how did you overtake the cyclist dangerously?
Answer: This is because you didn't check your mirrors and blind spots before overtaking.

Question: Kathleen, how did you cause the vehicle behind you to brake after pulling back in?
Answer: This is because you didn't check your rearview mirror before pulling back in.

SAFE DISTANCE

Question: Kathleen, why are you following the vehicle in front too closely (tailgating).
Answer: This is because you are not leaving a safe gap.

ADEQUATE CLEARANCE

Question: Kathleen, why did you pass the parked car too closely?
Answer: You were focussing your attention on the parked car.

Question: Kathleen, why did you pass the cycle too closely?
Answer: You were unaware the cyclist was about to negotiate a drain and move out.

ANTICIPATION OF PEDESTRIANS

Question: Kathleen, why did you put the pedestrians in a dangerous situation?
Answer: This is because you invited them to cross.

Question: Kathleen, why did you almost run the pedestrian over?
Answer: This is because you didn't anticipate them crossing.

ANTICIPATION OF CYCLISTS

Question: Kathleen, why did you have to swerve harshly as the cyclist swerved.
Answer: You didn't give the cyclist enough room as you passed.

Question: Kathleen, why did you not expect the cyclist to turn in front of you at the mini roundabout?

Answer: This is because the cyclist did not signal, and you assumed they were travelling straight on.

ANTICIPATION OF DRIVERS

Question: Kathleen, why did you attempt to pull out in front of the vehicle approaching with his left-hand signal on?
Answer: This is because you did not anticipate his speed on approach.

Question: Kathleen, why did you not expect the vehicle to turn right in front of you?
Answer: This is because you did not anticipate the vehicle could do that.

Question: Kathleen, why did you turn into the junction because another vehicle flashed their headlights?
Answer: This is because you did not anticipate who the signal was.

Q&A Giving correct signals

SIGNALLING

Question: Kathleen, why did you indicate in the wrong direction?
Answer: This is because you did not move the indicator stalk in the direction you intend to travel.

Question: Kathleen, why did the vehicle pulling off their driveway think you were turning right?
Answer: This is because you signalled right instead of left.

Question: Kathleen, why did the vehicle behind you not know your intentions?
Answer: This is because you signalled after you had turned.

Question: Kathleen, why did the vehicle pulling off their driveway think you were turning right?
Answer: This is because you signalled right instead of left.

Question: Kathleen, why did you hold up the traffic unnecessarily at the junction?
Answer: This is because you signalled left but failed to go when it was clear to do so.

Question: Kathleen, why was the vehicle behind you unsure of your intentions?
Answer: This is because you did not signal before you started slowing.

Question: Kathleen, why was the vehicle behind was unsure of your intentions?
Answer: This is because you signalled unnecessarily around the parked vehicle.

FLASHING OF HEADLIGHTS

Question: Kathleen, why did you flash your headlights incorrectly?
Answer: This is because you thought it was a signal to other motorists to proceed.

Question: Kathleen, why did you proceed dangerously?
Answer: This is because another vehicle flashed, and you thought it was for you.

BRAKE LIGHTS

Question: Kathleen, why did the following vehicle not know you were slowing?
Answer: This is because you didn't brake, only slowing with your gears.

Q&A Progress, hesitancy and normal stop position

PROGRESS TOO FAST

Question: Kathleen, why are you exceeding the speed limit?
Answer: This is because you are trying to keep up with the vehicles in front.

Question: Kathleen, are you making progress, but it is unnecessary?
Answer: This is because the traffic ahead is coming to a stop.

PROGRESS TOO SLOW

Question: Kathleen, why are you not making progress on the new road?
Answer: This is because you have emerged onto a faster speed limit road.

HESITANCY

Question: Kathleen, how did you confuse the vehicle behind you?
Answer: This is because you had plenty of time to emerge safely.

POSITION TOO WIDE

Question: Kathleen, how did you cause the vehicle on your right to brake on the roundabout?
Answer: This is because you did not position the car in your lane correctly and drifted into theirs.

POSITION TOO CLOSE

Question: Kathleen, why did you mount the kerb as you went around the roundabout?
Answer: This is because you did not position the car for turning.

Question: Kathleen, why did you mount the roundabout as you turned?
Answer: This is because you did not position the car correctly for turning right.

EMERGING

Question: Kathleen, why do you not have a good view of approaching traffic?
Answer: This is because you are too far from the give way lines.

Question: Kathleen, why are other vehicles having to move around you?
Answer: This is because you have not positioned the car behind the white lines whilst waiting to emerge.

POSITION RIGHT

Question: Kathleen, how are you confusing the following vehicle?

Answer: This is because you indicated right but are positioned as if you intend to turn left.

POSITION LEFT

Question: Kathleen, how are you confusing the vehicle behind?
Answer: This is because you indicated left but are positioned as if you intend to turn right.

PEDESTRIANS

Question: Kathleen, how did you put the pedestrians into a dangerous situation?
Answer: This is because you invited them to cross.

Q&A Comprehension of traffic signs

NOT NOTICING SPEED LIMIT SIGNS

Question: Kathleen, what is the speed limit on this road?
Answer: As you turned into the new junction, you did not look up to look for any speed limit changes.

Question: Kathleen, why have you have taken the wrong turning?
Answer: This is because you did not look at the signpost correctly.

TRAFFIC LIGHTS

Question: Kathleen, why did you cross the amber traffic light?
Answer: This is because you didn't check behind you on the approach to the green light and start slowing, anticipating it may change.

Question: Kathleen, why did you proceed on red and amber and not wait for the green light?
Answer: This is because you followed other road users. You must wait until the light is green and proceed if safe to do so.

Question: Kathleen, why didn't you slow down the temporary traffic lights?
Answer: This is because you didn't notice the Road Works sign on the approach.

TRAFFIC CONTROLLERS

Question: Kathleen, why didn't you slow earlier for the traffic controller?
Answer: This is because you didn't look ahead, see the traffic controller and be prepared to stop.

Question: Kathleen, why did you start slowing late for the traffic controller.
Answer: Do not wait until they have stepped into the road; you must stop as they put their sign out.

GIVE WAY SIGNS

Question: Kathleen, why were you going too fast approaching the give way?
Answer: This is because you didn't see the give way sign on the approach.

Question: Kathleen, why have you stopped too far from the give way sign?
Answer: This is because you didn't look at the give way lines on the approach.

Question: Kathleen, why have you stopped too far over the give way sign?

81

Answer: This is because you didn't look at the give way lines on the approach.

LANE DISCIPLINE

Question: Kathleen, why are you are in the wrong lane?
Answer: This is because you didn't look at the direction sign on the approach.

Question: Kathleen, why are you straddling the lane?
Answer: This is because you are not looking at the road markings.

Question: Kathleen, why did you attempt to enter a no-entry sign?
Answer: This is because you didn't look up when turning into a new junction and see the no-entry sign.

Copyright

The ADI Core Competencies (Approved Driving Instructor) Training Manual is the copyright of Kathleen Kirkland T/A Kathleen School of Motoring, Bletchley (Kathleen SOM). With payment by you for a copy of the ADI Core Competencies (Approved Driving Instructor) Training Manual, Kathleen SOM grants you the non-exclusive right to use the ADI Core Competencies Training Manual solely for your own personal or internal business purposes. You may not copy the ADI Core Competencies (Approved Driving Instructor) Training Manual to any third party or transfer or assign any of the copyright in the ADI Core Competencies (Approved Driving Instructor) Training Manual or grant any right over the ADI Core Competencies (Approved Driving Instructor) Training Manual.

Written and copyrighted to:
Kathleen Kirkland
DVSA ADI Grade A
ORDIT Registered Trainer
DVSA Fleet Registered Driver Trainer
Kathleen School of Motoring, Bletchley
Website: www.kathleensom.co.uk
Email: kathleesom@live.co.uk
Phone: 0800 24 25 26 9
Facebook: Driving School Milton Keynes, Kathleen School of Motoring
Milton Keynes, Bletchley

Printed in Great Britain
by Amazon